Attacking The Crown Jewels

ATTACKING

THE CROWN JEWELS

how to protect your business strategy
against competitive threats

PHIL BOOKMAN

ISBN: 1-4196-2592-6

Printed in the United States of America
First edition 2007

The names of all companies and products mentioned in this book are used for identification purposes only and may be trademarks or registered trademarks of their respective owners. The author disclaims any affiliation, association, ownership, sponsorship, endorsement by or connection with such owners.

Strategic Competitive Defense Planning[SM] is a service mark of the Crown Jewels Group.

BookSurge Publishing
Charleston, South Carolina
www.booksurge.com

*To Lois, always constant with patience,
encouragement and support.*

Contents

Part 1: Strategic Competitive Defense

Part 2: Strategic Competitive Defense Planning

Attacking The Crown Jewels

Attack away from the competitor's offering that threatens your strategy, the strategic threat.

Attack one of the competitor's offerings that is essential to its strategy, one of its crown jewels.

Attack with enough credibility that the competitor must defend its crown jewels by diverting resources away from the strategic threat, thus reducing or eliminating the threat to you.

Introduction

"Only the paranoid survive." – Andy Grove

Your business has been executing as planned. You've positioned yourself well against your competitors. But you've heard from the field that a different competitor is on the horizon: they have something new and it is squarely focused on your core business.

And your current strategy won't handle this menace.

You have a strategic competitive threat! The landscape has changed, and you need a new type of strategy to defend your business—your crown jewels—against this competition.

You need a strategic competitive defense.

Patterns emerge after studying how successful companies handle strategic competitive threats in the real world. Based on those patterns, *Attacking the Crown Jewels* offers a step-by-step process you can use to assess these threats, select the ones to focus on, and plan defenses against them. That process is called the Strategic Competitive Defense Planning^{SM} process.

These patterns also reveal a potent defense that has been used for a long time by many companies, but has not previously been named or modeled. *Attacking the Crown Jewels* does both. It is called "the crown jewels attack," and it gives you the power to shape the competitive landscape and influence your competitor's behavior to remove or reduce the threat you fear. The crown jewels attack and the more traditional defenses form the arsenal of weapons used in the Strategic Competitive Defense Planning process.

Your crown jewels are the products you offer that are so vital to your success that you must defend them at all costs. Competitive threats to your crown jewels are lurking everywhere. They will not just go away if you ignore them. There is no place to hide. So protect your crown jewels—attack theirs!

Part 1

Strategic Competitive Defense

"All strategy depends on competition." –
Bruce Henderson, founder, Boston Consulting Group

1

A Tale Of A Worried Man

"Competition is always a fantastic thing...
we've got some fantastic competitors and it keeps
us on our toes." – Bill Gates

I t is 1999 and you are Bill Gates. You have successfully,
though painfully, moved your lumbering giant of a
software company, Microsoft, into the Internet era and
trounced upstart Netscape Communications. Instead of
being thrilled or relieved that this titanic threat has been
overcome, you are a worried man.

You have learned from your friend Andy Grove that "only
the paranoid survive." You are now indeed paranoid.
Paranoid about game consoles. Your "we nearly missed the
Internet" experience has opened your eyes to other threats

to your Windows empire. You imagine how game consoles hooked to the Internet could doom your dream of Windows in the family room. Game consoles with internet access could evolve into being replacements for home computers using Windows.

Worse, Sony has emerged as the likely dominant game console player with its PlayStation product. Sony has deep pockets and extensive knowledge of the consumer enter- tainment and electronics business. They are too big and well established for you to try to crush them, like you did to Netscape. They do not fit with Microsoft strategically, so buying them is not an alternative worth considering. So you have decided to make a bold strategic move. You will make Sony defend PlayStation as a game console. You believe that this will divert Sony resources that could otherwise go into making PlayStation into a home PC replacement. You will do this by attacking PlayStation, one of Sony's crown jewels, with a Microsoft game console, which you refer to as the "X-box" (the hyphen will later be dropped by your marketing gurus).

Your engineers have convinced you that this machine must be designed from the ground up to be focused on games, with great graphics processing on TVs at its core. They have been clear that they mean both hardware and software. They have been bold enough to tell you flat out that this means no Windows under the hood. They have been persuasive and you have decided that the threat is great enough that it is time to abandon your "Windows Everywhere" mantra as long as you can keep game consoles *from becoming replacements for general purpose home computers where Windows rules.*

You are committing Microsoft to this Xbox strategy for the long term. You are willing to lose money and accept second or third place in the market for years so long as you keep PlayStation in its place as a mere game console. Windows must be defended at all costs. You believe that time, money, and constancy of focus and vision are on your side.

Fast forward to the present. Xbox is a $5 billion business and close to turning a profit. Microsoft and Sony are battling for the top spot in the game console space. Sony is tied up in knots keeping PlayStation competitive with Xbox in games, and its threat to replace home personal computers seems well contained. The multi-year Microsoft Xbox strategy is relentlessly moving forward, slowly but surely, step-by-step.

While one can only imagine what Bill Gate's might have been thinking, the Xbox strategy illustrates Microsoft at its strategic best. It defends Windows from a potential threat and adds a growth product line to Microsoft's portfolio. The plan to accomplish this illustrates a defensive strategy called *attacking the crown jewels.*

The objective of attacking the crown jewels is to divert a competitor's resources away from an existing or potential offering (a product or service aimed at a particular group of customers) that threatens your strategy, thus weakening or eliminating the threat. This is accomplished by attacking another offering, one that is crucial to the success of the competitor's strategy, one of its crown jewels that it must vigorously defend by redeploying its resources. The offering you fear is the *strategic threat* and the offering you attack with to defend against the strategic threat is called the *attack weapon.*

Attacking The Crown Jewels

Attack away from the competitor's offering that threatens your strategy, the strategic threat.

Attack one of the competitor's offerings that is essential to its strategy, one of its crown jewels.

Attack with enough credibility that the competitor must defend its crown jewels by diverting resources away from the strategic threat, thus reducing or eliminating the threat to you.

In the Xbox example, the strategic threat Microsoft was dealing with was a possible future Sony PlayStation that might evolve enough to compete with Windows PCs in the home. They chose to attack PlayStation in its then-current form, strictly a game console, one of Sony's most dazzling crown jewels. Microsoft believed that their resources and track record would make the Xbox threat credible to Sony. Thus, Sony would be forced to defend its game console by diverting resources away from efforts to make PlayStation a replacement for home computers using Windows.

The above summary of the crown jewels attack strategy is deceptively brief but it is far from simple. Chapters three and four delve into it in detail, and also present a comprehensive model for strategic competitive defense. To set the stage for that, the next chapter reviews how to identify competitive threats and determine which ones are truly dangerous enough that you must specifically and strategically defend against them.

The Strategic Defense Arsenal

Attacking the crown jewels is a companion strategy to the time-honored, traditional competitive defenses detailed in chapter three: Buy Them, Crush Them, Unleash The Lawyers, Erect Barriers To Entry, and Spread FUD. These traditional defenses have been extensively studied and well documented.

The Strategic Competitive Defense Arsenal

Attack Their Crown Jewels
- Classic Attack
- Proxy Attack
- Bamboozle Attack
- Jawbone Attack

Traditional Defenses
- Buy Them
- Crush Them
- Unleash The Lawyers
- Erect Barriers To Entry
- Spread FUD

The practice of attacking the crown jewels is not a new approach to competitive defense, but it has not been modeled before, nor has it been recognized as a cohesive, unified paradigm. The objective in developing the crown jewels attack model has been to make this strategy accessible and usable by any organization that is serious about defending its strategy against strategic threats posed by competition. Attacking the crown jewels is a powerful and often superior member of the strategic competitive defense arsenal.

The model of the crown jewels attack strategy presented in chapters three and four of this book has been developed by observing, analyzing and participating in the high-technology industry for three decades. Many of the examples used in this book describe real actions taken by well known high-technology companies. However, there is nothing inherently high-tech about the crown jewels attack strategy.

Nor do you have to be a giant company like Microsoft to use this strategy. Big company examples have been chosen to make them as familiar as possible to readers. You do not need to have the vast resources of a huge enterprise to attack the crown jewels. You do not need to be the leader in your market. What you do need is tenacity, focus, and sufficient resources to mount an attack your competitor will take seriously. Deep pockets are helpful, but they are neither necessary nor sufficient to get others to take your moves seriously. What matters is the quality of the threat the attack represents as perceived by the competitor.

About This Book

Attacking The Crown Jewels is about using a systematic, comprehensive approach to strategic competitive threat identification and defense. It shows when and how to protect your business strategy by attacking a threatening competitor's most important assets, its crown jewels, and how you can use your attack to grow your business. The book is divided into two parts.

Part one presents the concepts of competitive strategic defense, the crown jewels attack model and the more traditional competitive defenses.

- After this introductory first chapter, chapter two discusses the various kinds and sources of competitive threats, and how to recognize which threats are strategic.

- Chapter three deals with the specifics of the crown jewels attack strategy along with the traditional defenses that can be used against strategic competitive threats.

- Chapter four explains and illustrates the four distinct styles that can be used to attack the crown jewels: the Classic Attack, the Proxy Attack, the Bamboozle Attack, and the Jawbone Attack.

Part two of this book provides a process for planning and implementing strategic defensive attacks.

- Chapter five spells out a step-by-step process for strategic defense planning.

- Chapter six illustrates the process with a case study.

- Chapter seven discusses how to assure the success of attacking the crown jewels and similar strategic initiatives and closes with a call to action.

Competition is a fact of business life we cannot avoid. This book was written as part of a mission to help organizations become proactive and successful in meeting the challenges posed by strategic competition. You are encouraged to join in this quest.

2

Competitive Threats

"The other teams could make trouble for us
if they win." – Yogi Berra

A review of the sources and types of competitive threats sets the foundation for the crown jewels attack strategy, specifically, and strategic competitive defense in general. Competitors can come from many places and in many forms. They fall into three broad categories: direct competitors, indirect competitors, and potential competitors.

Direct And Indirect Competitors

Direct competitors are the most obvious competitive threats. They have the offerings that are similar enough to your offering that the prospective customer sees them as a group from which to choose. For example, Dell laptop computers and HP laptop computers are direct competitors.

Indirect competitors offer products or services that can be substituted for your offering or those of your direct competitors. Breakfast cereals, for example, compete indirectly with breakfast bars, pancakes, waffles, eggs, muffins and a host of other breakfast food choices. If do-it-yourself is a viable choice, it too is indirect competition. There are often many more indirect competitors than direct ones.

Back to the laptop computer example, what about Apple Macintosh laptops? Are they direct competitors for Dell and HP laptops that run Windows and not the Macintosh operating system? How about desktop computers from these and other vendors, are they direct competition for the laptops? Both of these questions illustrate the gray area between direct and indirect competitors. The distinction between direct and indirect competitors is not what is important. What matters is that you consider both kinds when planning your strategy so that you do not miss any.

Potential Competitors

There are many potential sources of new competitors. They can come from technology changes, as when VCRs and the video rental stores that fed them created an inexpensive home competitor to movie theaters. They can come from political changes, as when the fall of the Iron Curtain brought low cost Eastern European manufacturing into competition with plants in Western Europe.

A supplier may decide to bypass you and sell directly to the customer, thus becoming a new entrant. In its simplest form this is known as "cutting out the middleman" or disintermediation (removing the intermediary). Consider what happened to travel agents when airlines, hotel chains, and car rental companies began using the Internet to sell directly to consumers. In a few years, the travel agent industry shrank dramatically, perhaps permanently. When Oracle decided to enter the business applications software market, business applications vendors who saw Oracle as a supplier of the database they used in their products suddenly had a major new competitor on their hands.

Customers can also evolve into competitors. They may buy your product and then rent the use of it to others, thus depriving you of potential customers. Sometimes a customer will learn from you and later decide to compete directly or indirectly. This is often the unintended consequence of "technology transfer."

A potential competitive threat may be any directly or indirectly competing product or service you believe someone is likely to develop, and that a customer might choose instead of your offering. For example, Microsoft is a threat to IBM's complex enterprise technology solutions services business because Microsoft has all of the ingredients necessary to effectively attack this market. A potential threat may also be an existing product or service that is not a current strategic threat but that could evolve to become one. For example, Apple's Macintosh operating system is a potential threat to Microsoft Windows because Apple might decide to make it available on non-Apple personal computers instead of just on Macintosh computers. Similarly, as shown in chapter one, Sony's PlayStation is a potential threat to Microsoft Windows because it might evolve from a game console into a web browsing appliance.

Competitive Self-Delusion

The only one who can correctly determine if something is, or could become, a competitive offering is a prospective customer. Others may have beliefs and opinions, but prospective customers are the source of truth. This simple fact is often overlooked and the set of competitors is frequently too narrowly defined because of a psychological syndrome called "competitive self-delusion."

Competitive self-delusion is the state you are in when you fool yourself about the true nature of the competitive landscape. As with most such syndromes, it fulfills certain psychological needs. The most common ones are a desire to have less to worry about, a yearning to feel good about your company and its offerings, and a longing to think about getting rich instead of how to cope with another irritating threat.

There are several symptoms of competitive self-delusion. The most common one is being in a state of denial, usually accompanied by believing your own marketing hype. For example, many traditional software companies faced with open-source competition proclaimed to the world various reasons that free software developed mainly by volunteers would never compete with traditional software products from traditional companies. Those organizations that believed their own messages about this delayed planning and executing defenses against this threat and gave open-source competition time to become well established, if not entrenched.

Another symptom of competitive self-delusion occurs when you get evidence, often superficial, that leads to a conclusion that pleases you, and do not dig deeper so you do not risk finding contrary evidence. It can happen like this. You ask your sales and marketing staff, "do we ever compete with XYZ?" They tell you they rarely run into XYZ in actual customer situations. You conclude that XYZ is not a significant competitor. Sadly for you, certain aspects of your offering exclude you early from those situations in which you lose to XYZ, and vice-versa. For example, if you sell your product and XYZ is rented, those looking for a rental will eliminate your product from consideration right from the start. That may be fine if your strategy is intentionally to only sell and never rent, but it is a mistake if you can find a way to satisfy those customers who prefer to rent without compromising your strategy.

A different symptom of competitive self-delusion occurs when you evaluate potential threats exclusively by thinking about them yourself and discussing them within an in-group in your own organization and external industry experts and analysts. This form of expert-group navel-gazing creates an insulated, ivory tower effect.

26 Attacking The Crown Jewels

The cure for competitive self-delusion is to methodically and dispassionately identify competitors by doing the following:

1. Define your prospective customers as broadly as possible.

2. Frequently, systematically, and in many ways, discover the set of offerings your prospects consider when they first *begin* thinking about filling the need your offering satisfies.

3. Frequently, systematically, and in many ways, test how your visionary and early-adopter prospects respond to *potential* threats that may in the future fill the need your offering satisfies.

Be particularly careful when you seek feedback from prospective customers about potential threats, where competitive self-delusion can easily limit the value of your data and cloud your judgment. With a potential threat, it is essential that you test the concept of the threat on prospects, broadly defined, not just the so-called industry experts. How would they react to a theoretical offering with certain attributes from a certain source? It is critical, however, to ask this of the right prospects. Focus on visionaries and early adopters who can truly imagine the value of an offering that does not yet exist. This means discovering how to find these people in the general population of prospective customers and then asking them the right questions, a task for marketing specialists. Often, this requires using external experts to get unbiased results.

Broadly defining prospects for the purpose of competitive analysis is distinct from the approach used in your more short-term focused product marketing and sales strategies, which likely narrowly define and target prospective customer segments. These are two different activities. Feedback from your marketing and sales efforts that are applied to producing current and near-term results from market segments is but one source of input to the ongoing strategic marketing process of gathering competitive market intelligence.

Competitive Self-Delusion

Symptoms:

- Denial
- Believing your own hype
- "We rarely run into them" myopia
- Ignoring early exclusion from consideration
- Ivory tower navel-gazing

Cure:

- Define prospective customers as broadly as possible
- Frequently, systematically and in many ways, discover the offerings prospects consider when they first *begin* thinking about filling the need your offering satisfies
- Frequently, systematically and in many ways, test how visionary and early adopter prospects respond to *potential* threats that may in the future fill the need your offering satisfies

---

Competitive self-delusion is a common executive condition. The important thing is to recognize it and treat it in its early acute stages. If it becomes chronic, it can be terminal—to careers, if not companies.

Strategic Threats

The list of direct, indirect, and potential competitive threats can be dauntingly long indeed. Still, it is best to first cast a wide net when developing the list. After the list is complete, the next step is to decide which of the threats is strategic by evaluating the severity, robustness, and credibility of each of them. A threat is strategic if and only if all three of these criteria are sufficiently met. Chapter five provides a process and worksheet for evaluating competitive threats using these attributes. Here, they are discussed in more general terms.

Severe

A threat is considered severe if it may prevent you from reaching your business plan's key strategic objectives. These objectives are usually stated in terms of revenue, profit, and market share, but you may come up with others that are subject to competitive threat. Three to five years is generally a good strategic planning horizon. Less, and you are probably being myopic and not looking far enough ahead. More, and you may be dreaming instead of doing strategic planning.

Robust

Severity alone is not enough to make a threat strategic. It must also be robust, that is, it must be essentially unaffected by your routine competitive processes and strategies. Handling such a threat therefore requires that you develop a strategy that targets it specifically, or that you modify your routine approaches to encompass this type of threat.

Strategic Threats

A threat is strategic if it is severe, robust, and credible

Severe: It may prevent you from reaching your business plan's strategic objectives

Robust: It is essentially unaffected by your routine competitive processes and strategies

Credible: If existing, it will likely endure
If potential, it will likely occur

Routine competitive processes and strategies include those for sales, marketing, and development. These should handle most competitive threats. If you find that not to be the case, if you have a significant number of threats that appear to be robust, re-examine these competitive processes and strategies. Align them with the realities of your market before you contemplate planning new individual strategic defenses.

Credible

If a threat is severe and robust, it still may not merit a strategic intervention. The third and final hurdle is that the threat must be credible. Rating a threat's credibility calls for an assessment of the likelihood that an existing threat will endure, or that a potential threat will actually occur. There are many things to consider in making this judgment. How important is the revenue and profit of the offering to the competitor's strategy? How likely is the offering to gain market traction? How likely is the competitor to stay focused on the offering? How financially strong is the competitor? Is the competitor the acquisition target of a company that might more effectively exploit its offering?

Each threat that you determine is strategic, that meets your threshold measure of severity, robustness, and credibility, commands an action plan to reduce or eliminate it. Set that threshold high enough to assure that you are developing strategic defensive initiatives for only those competitive threats that truly put your strategy in jeopardy. The rest of the threats on your list form a watch list that is used as input for the next time you review competitive threats.

The next chapter looks at the specifics of attacking the crown jewels and other defenses that can be used against strategic competitive threats.

3

Strategic Defenses

"Attack is the best form of defense." – proverb

Once you have identified your strategic competitive threats, it is time to develop a defensive action plan to deal with each of them. Otherwise, all you have done is create a management worry list. This chapter reviews the defenses that can be used against these threats. These are Attack Their Crown Jewels and the traditional defensive competitive strategies: Buy Them, Crush Them, Unleash The Lawyers, Erect Barriers To Entry, and Spread FUD. The discussion starts with the strategy for which this book is named.

Attack Their Crown Jewels

The practice of attacking the crown jewels is not at all new, but it has not previously been integrated into a framework that can be systematically used for strategic competitive defense. The model presented in this book shows the various forms this powerful defense can take, which are called *attack styles*. These attack styles—the Classic Attack, the Proxy Attack, the Bamboozle Attack, and the Jawbone Attack—are discussed in detail in the next chapter. They are united by their common method and objective. The method is to attack an offering that is one of the competitor's crown jewels. The objective is to cause your competitor to divert resources away from the offering that threatens you, the *strategic threat,* to defend the crown jewels you attack. With fewer resources available to it, the threat is reduced or eliminated. This is sometimes called starving the threat.

All competitors have limited resources, and it is the job of senior management to allocate them to meet the needs of the business. These resources include money, time, and management attention. Other resources are factories, labor, land, energy, raw materials, and supplies, though it can be argued that in most cases these can be acquired given enough money and time.

How do you get the competitor to redeploy its resources the way you desire? This is accomplished by aggressively attacking another offering of the competitor, one that is essential to its strategy, one of its crown jewels. For example, you may launch a new or enhanced product or service, the attack weapon, that competes with the crown jewels in a manner that convinces the competitor that it better apply considerable resources to defend itself.

Because the crown jewels you attack represent something that the competitor is already good at, the law of diminishing returns often works in your favor. As applied in this situation, this means that the better an offering is, the more you have to spend proportionally for each increment of improvement. Therefore, as your competitor strives to bolster its already strong offering, it finds that it has to apply ever greater levels of resources for marginal gains.

Chapter one summarized the crown jewels attack strategy as follows:

- Attack away from the competitor's offering that threatens your strategy, the strategic threat.

- Attack one of the competitor's offerings that is essential to its strategy, one of its crown jewels.

- Attack with enough credibility that the competitor must defend its crown jewels by diverting resources away from the strategic threat, thus reducing or eliminating the threat to you.

When Microsoft attacked Sony PlayStation with Xbox, it attacked away from the strategic threat, "PlayStation as a home PC replacement." It chose "PlayStation as a game console" to attack, one of Sony's crown jewels. It attacked with fanfare, counting on its reputation as a tenacious competitor with patience, focus, and deep pockets, to persuade Sony to defend "PlayStation as a game console" and PlayStation has not evolved into a home personal computer replacement.

Selecting The Crown Jewels To Attack

To implement the crown jewels attack strategy, you must decide which of the competitor's crown jewels to attack. When doing so, it is important to think about the competitor's offerings with sufficient granularity.

An offering is a product or service aimed at a particular market segment. A market segment is a group of customers identified by common buying behavior. Consumer segmentation can include many factors, such as geography, age, gender, life-stage, marital status, education, avocation, and income. Business markets can be segmented by geography, company size, industry, business function, desire for customization, and other factors that shape buyer needs and expectations. A particular product or service can be packaged in such a way that it appeals to the general market, in which case it is called an *undifferentiated* offering. A *differentiated* offering is packaged to appeal to one or more specific market segments.

The automobile industry is a good example of consumer segmentation. The basic product is packaged in terms of price, quality, styling, accessories, and other details to target a wide variety of market segments. Lexus and other premium luxury models are aimed at the well-to-do, mature customer. Prius and other hybrid vehicles appeal to the consumer concerned about the environment and fuel costs. Models are aimed at young families, outdoor enthusiasts, affluent men, single mothers, commuters, city drivers, and a myriad of finely defined segments based on a large matrix of factors.

Choosing which of the competitor's crown jewels to target depends on the nature of the threat. If the strategic threat you want to defend against is from an existing offering in its current form, then aim the attack at something else.

If instead the threat is that an existing offering could potentially evolve into a strategic threat, you have two choices for a pre-emptive attack. You can attack another existing offering. Alternatively, you can attack the offering in its current form. In either case, the objective is to keep it in its current form, preventing it from changing in the way you fear.

Selecting The Crown Jewels To Attack

If the threat is...	Then attack...
An existing offering in its current form	Another existing strategic offering
An existing offering because of how it might potentially evolve	The offering in its current form or another existing strategic offering
A potential new offering	An existing strategic offering

As seen in chapter one, this is what happened when Microsoft used Xbox to attack Sony PlayStation as a game console. The outcome of this attack has been to keep PlayStation from evolving into a home computer replacement. On the other hand, you can attack another of the competitor's crown jewels to divert resources completely away from the threat. When Microsoft attacked iPod/iTunes with Zune, the result was to divert Apple's resources away from possibly freeing the Macintosh operating system to run on non-Apple computers, in direct competition with Windows.

With a purely potential threat posed by a possible new offering, you can consider pre-emptively attacking any of the competitor's current crown jewels. IBM attacked Microsoft Windows by throwing its support behind the Linux open-source operating system to deter Microsoft from becoming a more focused competitor in the arena of IBM's core strategic business, complex enterprise technology solutions.

One situation that presents particular challenges is the pure-play competitor. A pure-play competitor is one that has only one offering, the one that directly (not potentially) threatens your strategy. Pure-play competitors can be the most dangerous because of the focus they bring to their offering and their utter dependence on its success. There is no other offering for you to attack, nothing to which you can divert your competitor's attention and resources. This condition makes them effectively invulnerable to the crown jewels attack strategy. Later in this chapter, strategic defenses other than attacking the crown jewels are presented. These can be used against a strategic threat from a pure-play competitor.

A competitor's differentiated offering of a product or service in one market segment may be a good choice as the target when that same product or service offered in another segment is itself the strategic threat. This can be especially helpful when dealing with a competitor that appears to be pure-play. If their offering is differentiated, they may not be pure-play at all when you consider each segment separately. Thus, you may be able to attack away from the threat by attacking away from the segment(s) for which you both significantly compete.

Suppose, for example, that your company, Snick Snack, is in the business of providing healthy, low calorie, low fat snacks for children under the Snickys brand. You target mothers concerned about their children's health in general, and obesity specifically. One of your major competitors, Mega Cookie, offers Mega Bites, an assortment of healthy, low calorie, low fat cookies aimed at the same market segment. Rumor has it that Mega Cookie is considering expanding their healthy cookie business to add other healthy treats. After careful evaluation, you conclude that this potential threat is strategic and want to plan a strategic defense against it.

Healthy cookies are Mega Cookie's only current product line. This seems like head-to-head competition. However, unlike Snick Snack that markets exclusively to mothers and their children, Mega Cookie has a second major offering. It also targets Mega Bites at overweight adults. This market segment is a major source of its revenue.

Mega Cookie's crown jewels are not healthy cookies. Its crown jewels are "healthy cookies targeted at mothers and children" and "healthy cookies targeted at overweight adults." Snick Snack can therefore consider developing an attack targeting healthy cookies targeted at overweight adults. The objective of this attack would be to induce Mega Cookies to defend Mega Bites targeted at overweight adults, diverting resources it might otherwise expend on enhancing or expanding its products targeted at children and their mothers.

There may be several viable crown jewels that could be targeted. Since you want the competitor to change its behavior as a result of the attack, the most important thing to consider when choosing a target is the impact of the attack on the competitor. Your attack must be perceived as extremely threatening, so pick a target where a significant new threat will really matter to the competitor. Do not just pile on where your competitor is already under siege. Do attack where the competitor has little effective strategic competition. Microsoft's Xbox attack on Sony's PlayStation strongly influenced Sony's behavior because, except for Nintendo, it had weak competition. If PlayStation already had several strong competitors, the Xbox attack would not have altered the competitive landscape enough to change Sony's behavior very much.

In addition to choosing from among possible targets, there are also several ways to mount an attack, known as attack styles. Part two of this book, as part of the overall strategic competitive defense planning process, offers a step-by-step methodology for selecting the target and style for an attack.

When To Attack The Crown Jewels

Consider using the crown jewels attack strategy when the threat is strategic, there are viable crown jewels to target, you have staying power, and the competitor's likely response is tolerable. Determining strategic threats was explored in depth in chapter two and crown jewels attack targets were discussed in the previous section. Staying power and the competitor's likely response are discussed in the next two sections of this chapter.

When To Attack The Crown Jewels

The threat is strategic:	It is severe, robust, and credible
There is a viable target:	You can effectively attack away from the strategic threat
You have staying power:	You have the resources, focus, and tenacity to sustain the attack for as long as it is needed
The likely response is acceptable:	You are prepared to handle the competitor's most likely reaction

---

Part two of this book explains how to analyze threats using all of the above criteria and then how to develop appropriate defensive attacks as part of the overall strategic competitive defense planning process.

Staying Power

A successful crown jewels attack requires staying power. Staying power is about having the resources, focus, and tenacity to sustain the attack for as long as it is needed.

40 Attacking The Crown Jewels

You do not have to be a giant company with deep pockets to have staying power. As shown in the next chapter, there are a number of attack styles that can be used, each with different levels of cost. Staying power has more to do with management commitment and continuity of strategic direction than with company size or wealth. Chapter seven of this book looks at steps that can be taken to boost staying power and assure the success of defensive strategies.

Assess Competitor's Likely Response

Before choosing a crown jewels attack, carefully evaluate the competitor's likely response to be sure the probable outcomes are desirable or at least tolerable. An ill-considered attack may result in the competitor becoming even more of a strategic threat.

For example, Dell's entry into the printer market attacked rival HP's crown jewels, laser and inkjet printers. Dell and HP were already competing for market leadership in computers. The printer attack backfired because HP was already committed to heavy investment in its computer crown jewels, as signaled by its Compaq acquisition, and would not be diverted. If anything, the attack only served to focus HP's troops more on Dell as an enemy, daring to attack their precious printers. So carefully consider how the competitor has reacted to past threats and what you would do if you were its CEO facing the prospective attack. Then imagine how you in return would handle each scenario. Are you prepared to cope with the most likely ones? Would your attack actually divert their resources as you desire, away from the threat? Or would it increase your vulnerability?

Choose an attack target where you can not only mount an effective, sustained attack, but where you are ready, willing, and able to handle the likely response.

Attack Away From The Threat

The objective of attacking the crown jewels is to divert your competitor's resources away from the offering that threatens your strategy. It is a serious mistake to lose sight of the word "divert." This is what occurs when the crown jewels attack concept is oversimplified, and a head-to-head attack is used against the threat.

In *Sun Tzu and the Art of Business*, Mark McNeilly shows how to apply the strategic military principals handed down from the ancient Chinese general Sun Tzu to modern business. Sun Tzu warned against a strategy of head-to-head attack against the enemy's strength. This, he said, leads to a war of attrition that exhausts the resources of both sides of the conflict.

This thinking applies to business when two or more direct competitors get into head-to-head competition in a commoditized market. *Commoditized* means that all offerings are pretty much equal in value delivered to the customer. No one is successfully innovating with respect to the offering to achieve competitive advantage. The only differentiators becomes price and delivery. This tends to drive prices down, removing all of the profit from the market for all of the players. This is the analogue of Sun Tzu's war of attrition.

42 Attacking The Crown Jewels

The airline industry, a market comprised mainly of pure-play competitors competing primarily on price and schedule, illustrates this problem. Since 1980, while individual companies have had their ups and downs, the industry as a whole has never made enough profit to even cover its cost of capital and it historically operates at a net loss. Newcomers may profitably exploit niches but rarely sustain a differentiating competitive advantage for more than a few years. Cycles of bankruptcies and mergers are routine events. The commoditized airline industry has been drained of profit.

As the airline industry exemplifies, a common outcome of commoditization in a market is industry consolidation, where the ability to finance and manage the acquisition and integration of competitors becomes the essential capability. This is what happened in the business applications software market after the dot-com bubble burst in 2000. Oracle became an industry consolidator, leading with multi-billion dollar purchases of rivals PeopleSoft and Siebel Systems. By the end of 2006, Oracle had acquired over twenty companies. As Oracle CEO Larry Ellison said in a *BusinessWeek* article: "History repeats itself. It happened in railroads and cars. Now it's happening in software. And there, we're the consolidator."

The primary lesson here is that "attacking the crown jewels" means "attack away from the threat." It does not mean "attack the threat head-on." The secondary lesson is that successful "routine" competitive strategy comes from a mix of differentiating innovation and both direct and indirect attacks against the competitors in a market.

The Traditional Defenses

The traditional competitive defenses can be grouped into the following categories: Buy Them, Crush Them, Unleash The Lawyers, Erect Barriers To Entry, and Spread FUD. These defenses are called traditional because they have been studied, categorized, and documented for quite some time. Each of these has its own set of advantages and disadvantages.

Buy Them

There is no more certain way to remove a competitive threat than to buy the threatening company. As a bonus, you may harvest a revenue stream, customers, market segment access and expertise, technology, and/or key employees. This is commonly called "taking out a competitor." Corporate boards and the financial community are usually very comfortable with this strategy, especially when the rationale is expressed in terms of operational synergies, the numbers appear to back that up, and the price of the acquisition is right.

This strategy is recommended for consideration by companies that are unlikely to have the perseverance to use the crown jewels attack strategy. It is also a favorite choice against pure-play competitors. For example, Oracle's multi-billion dollar acquisitions of Peoplesoft and Seibel Systems removed two major enterprise business application competitors while strengthening Oracle in its competition against market leader SAP.

Attempting an acquisition defense has a number of inherent risks and potential stumbling blocks. It may be difficult and time consuming to find a price agreeable to buyer and seller. The methodical investigation process of due diligence may reveal significant problems with doing a deal for a wide range of reasons. If the attack is unfriendly, it can turn into a long and expensive battle. Another bidder may emerge victorious, realigning the competitive landscape in an undesirable way. Costly and time consuming regulatory issues may arise and may block the deal. Integrating the acquired company can be difficult and distracting. These are only some of the hazards that cause most acquisition attempts to fail to produce their expected benefits.

Crush Them

As discussed earlier in this chapter, Sun Tzu warned against head-to-head attacks against an enemy's strength. Instead, he advocated attacking weakness "where the enemy is most vulnerable." The idea is to attack the vulnerability relentlessly, with vastly superior and overwhelming force and crush the enemy. While attacking the crown jewels is intended to distract your competitor, this is a direct, head-on attack strategy called Crush Them.

In 1995, Microsoft adopted this defense against Netscape Communications. Netscape had a near monopoly in the web browser market. Microsoft, which had been slow in appreciating the significance of the Internet, woke up and recognized that the web browser could replace the operating system desktop as the delivery mechanism for many applications. This would force Windows, Microsoft's monopoly operating system, into a background role. In addition to the web browser, Netscape offered web server products, used to store and deliver web content to users. This threatened the network server versions of Windows. Netscape seemed to be coming at Microsoft Windows from all directions and had to be stopped.

Microsoft chose to crush Netscape, or, in a quote attributed to a then senior Microsoft executive, "cut off Netscape's air supply." Netscape was a pure-play competitor. As such, as discussed earlier in this chapter, Netscape was immune to a strategy designed to divert its resources like a crown jewels attack. This was because the threats to Microsoft were Netscape's only crown jewels, the web browser and server products. These were in fact its only sources of revenue. Microsoft attacked by offering its own web browser, Internet Explorer, for free, ultimately delivering it as just another part of Windows. Microsoft also began bundling free web server capability into Windows. Netscape found itself competing with free Microsoft products. It is not easy to compete with free.

To make matters worse for Netscape. Microsoft exploited a second vulnerability, distribution. While users had to choose to download and install Netscape products, Microsoft put the Internet Explorer icon front-and-center on the Windows desktop. This made the choice of using the Microsoft browser a "no-brainer" for Windows users, just like using the radio that comes with your car is an easy and obvious choice. This was very effective for personal computer users, where Windows owned 95% of the market. Microsoft similarly made its web server an easy choice for Windows server customers, ultimately even making a version of it freely available for all Windows users. It is not easy to compete with something your customers already have, know they have and that is always just a click away.

Microsoft threw its vast resources behind these web products, rapidly and constantly improving them, to assure that its free Windows components would be as good or better than Netscape's products. Netscape quickly went from being the primary source for web browsers and servers to being a replacement option for free parts of Windows, without compelling feature and function advantages. This head-to-head attack was relentless. Netscape's "air supply," its revenue, plummeted, as did its market share, and it never recovered. Three years after Microsoft's attack began, AOL acquired Netscape. It turned out that what AOL got out of the deal was mainly a brand name. For all intents and purposes, Netscape was dead, crushed by Microsoft.

This head-on attack strategy carries significant risks. One risk, which Microsoft discovered, is that the courts may later punish the attacker for predatory antitrust practices. Microsoft ultimately settled two such suits related to Netscape, one of which resulted in a consent decree with the U.S. Department of Justice curtailing certain Microsoft business practices, and another that saw Microsoft pay AOL $750 million.

Another risk is that you may severely damage but fail to destroy the competitor. Having shown the competitor its weaknesses and your strengths, the competitor may go away, lick its wounds, learn, and adapt. It may ultimately emerge stronger, wiser, and more formidable. Thus, gains from attacking weakness can be impressive in the short term but ultimately may backfire and produce a better competitor. You must really crush them for this strategy to be effective.

For example, in 1986 semiconductor giant Intel wanted to crush competition from its much smaller rival Advanced Micro Devices (AMD). In 1981, IBM had announced its new personal computer, the IBM PC, powered by the Intel 8086 microprocessor. IBM insisted on having a second manufacturing source, and so in 1982 Intel had entered into an agreement with AMD that allowed AMD to produce 8086 microprocessors (and, shortly thereafter, 80286 microprocessors for the IBM PC AT model). By 1986, AMD had evolved from a convenient second source manufacturer into a potential strategic threat. That threat was that AMD might improve on Intel's designs, producing Intel-compatible microprocessors that provided the market with a superior price-performance alternative to Intel's own offerings.

The manufacturers of IBM PC compatible computers (PC clones), led by Compaq, had reduced IBM's power in its dealings with Intel, and Intel saw no need to license second source manufacturers any longer. Intel had learned from IBM's mistakes that had allowed the rise of the IBM PC clone industry. It did not want to facilitate an Intel clone industry. So Intel cancelled the licensing agreement with AMD. At the same time, Intel was releasing its next generation of PC microprocessors, the 80386. Intel figured that, without the ability to produce 80386 microprocessors,

48 Attacking The Crown Jewels

AMD would soon be out of the PC microprocessor business and the threat would be crushed.

AMD took legal action to force Intel to honor what AMD saw as its contractual rights to information on Intel's 80386 technology. Intel aggressively pursued this complex series of suits and appeals. Ultimately, AMD realized that it would be better able to compete with Intel by reverse-engineering Intel's new microprocessors using what is known as a "clean room" approach. This method has a team of engineers document the way the original micro-processor works (if you give it certain inputs, it produces certain outputs). A second team then designs a new microprocessor that produces the same results given the same inputs as the original microprocessor, but without any access to the original microprocessor, its internal specifications or its documentation.

AMD released its own 80386 type microprocessor in 1991, and it was successful in the marketplace. This gave AMD staying power in the PC microprocessor market. In 1994, the California supreme court ruled that AMD was entitled to technical information from Intel on the 80386, but this would have been too little, too late had AMD either just waited for it hopefully or exited the PC microprocessor market in the interim.

Intel had failed to crush AMD. Instead, it taught AMD precisely what it originally wanted to avoid, that AMD's future success was in not merely cloning Intel microproc-essors but improving upon them while remaining compati-ble. Intel had attacked AMD's weakness, its dependence on Intel for design. AMD subsequently developed its own designs, often besting Intel in price-performance, and continues as a fierce and able competitor.

So crush them if you can, but be aware of the risks of legal action if you succeed and a strengthened competitor if you fail.

Unleash The Lawyers

This strategy boils down to filing legal action of some sort, like for patent or copyright infringement or antitrust violations, or getting the government to do it for you. The duration, cost, and outcome of legal action is inherently uncertain. It is easy to win the battle but lose the war. A well-heeled competitor can ward off a legal attack for a very long time, as AMD found in its legal maneuvering against Intel. Even if successful, good lawyering by the other side can dampen the outcome of the action so that the original strategic defensive objective is not met.

Even when successful legally, this defense rarely produces the desired strategic results and often signals the start of a death spiral in those companies who rely on it exclusively. For example, in 2003 the SCO Group, a company that owned certain intellectual property rights to the Unix operating system, filed a multi-billion dollar trade secrets suit against IBM in an attempt to protect Unix from the rise of the open-source Linux operating system. SCO alleged that IBM had used Unix code in parts of Linux, and warned companies that they had severe legal exposure if they used Linux. This legal donnybrook continues, with many of the claims tossed out by a federal judge. It has had no appreciable impact on Linux adoption but has cost SCO time, money, and distraction it could ill afford.

Another example of the bad omen of unleashing the lawyers instead of employing any other substantive defensive strategy is the 1998 federal antitrust action against Microsoft instigated at least in part by Netscape Communications, which did nothing to help prevent Netscape's demise.

All this is not to say that legitimate legal disputes should not be pursued. Make that judgment on its own merits on a case-by-case basis. However, relying primarily on using lawyers to mount a strategic defense against a competitive threat has such a low success rate that alarms should go off in the board room of any company considering its use for that purpose.

Erect Barriers To Entry

A barrier to entry is something that increases the risk for someone entering your market by creating a high initial entry cost. The idea is to convince a potential competitor that this will be a sunk cost, one they will not recover should they decide to later withdraw from the market. There are many such barriers. Here are some examples:

- Owning key intellectual property rights, such as drug and technology patents, like SCO's Unix intellectual property claims

- Creating high R&D and related costs by bundling many capabilities into and around the offering (often called "raising the bar") as

Microsoft did with its Office suite and with the
Windows operating system

- Achieving exclusive control of channels, as
  Microsoft has with Windows pre-installed by
  most personal computer manufacturers

- Owning scarce resources, like oil fields, gold
  mines, and diamond mines

- Owning exclusive operating licenses, like
  television broadcast channels

- Achieving economies of scale, as Wal-Mart and
  Intel have done

- Conditioning the market to expect an extensive,
  expensive advertising presence, as Apple has
  done with its iPod advertising, making any
  competitor that does not also have a strong
  advertising presence appear to be a second-tier
  player

- Creating high switching costs for customers, as
  Apple did for iPod by making the process
  required to play iTunes purchases on other
  MP3 players so complicated and error-prone
  that most customers would need to repurchase
  their music if they wanted to switch from iPod
  to another brand of player

- Creating high exit costs, as the National Football League did by establishing the practice of offering long-term contracts to star players, forcing new entrants like the World Football League to commit to long-term obligations to attract star talent

Every business wants to erect barriers to entry for all competitors, potential and existing. For existing competitors, you might call this "barriers to continuing." This defense is most often used as part of general strategy instead of being used against a specific threat. In the case of defending against a specific strategic threat, you seek to erect one or more new barriers that would discourage the threatening company from taking the course of action you fear. This can work for existing as well as potential competitors. A new barrier may cause an existing competitor to decide to divert resources to other product lines because the cost of continuing to compete with you has become too high.

In the 1980s, Apple's Macintosh operating system, with its graphical user interface (GUI), gave it a distinct competitive advantage over Microsoft's character-based DOS interface. To hamper Microsoft's efforts to develop its own GUI, Apple attempted to erect an intellectual property rights barrier, asserting copyright ownership of the "look and feel" of its interface. This included 189 specific elements, like the use of icons, rectangular windows and overlapping windows. Apple then licensed Microsoft the rights to use certain of these elements, but with severe limitations. For example, Microsoft was not permitted to use a trash can metaphor for deleting files, and windows had to be arranged side-by-side ("tiled") and not over-lapped. These restrictions made the first release of Microsoft Windows clunky and it was notably unsuccessful. That was Apple's intention.

Microsoft fought back by re-interpreting its license agreement with Apple and pretty much ignoring any restrictions. The Windows GUI soon became very Mac-like. In a series of legal actions starting in 1988, Apple attempted to assert copyright and contractual violations by Microsoft, finally dropping all claims in 1997 when Microsoft invested $150 million in Apple. In the interim, Windows achieved monopoly status, generating billions of dollars of annual revenue, and the payment to Apple was a trifle to Microsoft. Apple's barriers to entry strategy was an abject failure. This illustrates a major weakness of the intellectual property barriers to entry defense. It usually turns into an unleash the lawyers defense, with all of that strategy's inherent pitfalls.

The raise-the-bar barrier to entry strategy is designed to create a new weakness for one or more competitors by redefining a product or service genre. Ask this question: What can you do that will expand the customer's definition of your offering in such a way that it will discourage or distract the threatening company from taking the course of action you fear? This can include improvements you make to your offering, like increasing the breadth-and-depth of features and functions. It works best when it goes well beyond that and redefines the category in a manner that makes it very expensive and time-consuming for the competitor to respond. One way to do this is to develop ancillary products and services that increase the attractiveness of your offering, like online training services and local expert installation and support.

The Microsoft Office suite was a 1989 raise-the-bar action by Microsoft to defend its strategic plan for Excel and Word against threats from Lotus 1-2-3 and WordPerfect. Customers began expecting a suite of productivity applications. (Lotus 1-2-3 was never really much more than "Lotus 1." It was mainly a great spreadsheet program, but it did give Microsoft the suite idea.) Lotus and WordPerfect responded with all sorts of distracting, resource consuming activities that led to the death of the threats Microsoft feared.

When you raise the bar against a direct competitor, you attack a current weakness of its offering or create a new one. However, the risk of attacking an offering's weakness alone is that you will encourage the competitor to shore up the weakness and thus become a stronger competitor. This is why this approach is often used in combination with a crown jewels attack, which targets another offering and is intended to distract the competitor and divert its resources.

Most barriers to entry carry a common potential downside, the tradeoff between ongoing costs and customer perceived value. The expense of erecting and maintaining a barrier to entry can, over time, inflate your cost structure while adding little or no marginal value for customers. This in turn makes you vulnerable to a low cost entrant who strips the offering to its essentials. The upstart can then sell the core product or service at a much lower price, often targeting only those customer segments that are satisfied with the basic offering and are motivated primarily by price.

This can even happen on an industry-wide basis, as it has in the airline industry, where the key competitive issues are price and schedule. Low cost entrants like Southwest Airlines jettisoned meal service, in-flight movies, assigned seating, travel agents, VIP lounges, first-class and business-class cabins, and global route networks that the traditional carriers had seen as raise-the-bar barriers to entry. Focusing on the segment of the market that values cost over schedule convenience, they built a low cost structure into every aspect of their operations and business models from the start. The discount carriers unabashedly compete on low prices that the traditional airlines cannot match for a sustained period of time because they carry a much higher base cost structure. As of 2006, traditional airlines like American, United, Delta, and Continental continue to struggle to reduce costs, but the costs are so deeply embedded that these efforts take many years and often cannot be sufficiently accomplished even with the drastic step of a major merger and/or bankruptcy.

The lesson here is to be keenly aware of the balance between the ongoing cost structure impact of erecting and maintaining a barrier to entry and its ultimate influence on prices and customer perceived value.

56 Attacking The Crown Jewels

Spread FUD

Sowing Fear, Uncertainty, and Doubt (FUD) involves sending a consistent message that bad things may happen if you buy from the competitor but you are safe buying from us. While FUD as a tactic is often broadly targeted, as epitomized during the '60s, '70s, and '80s in the then popular aphorism, "No one ever got fired for buying from IBM," the FUD defensive strategy is aimed at a specific strategic threat.

For example, Microsoft launched a concerted FUD campaign against the open-source operating system Linux, starting in 1999 with an "it doesn't perform or scale well and may not be secure" message. In 2001 the appeal was changed to values, characterizing Linux as communistic and cancerous (to intellectual property rights). In 2002, the message was that support and other costs made free Linux a loser compared to Windows on the basis of total cost of ownership. In 2003, concerns about intellectual property took center stage after a small company called SCO began threatening legal action, asserting that code it owned had found its way into Linux illegally. Microsoft then began issuing various statements designed to make people nervous about their legal exposure if they used Linux. This may have slowed, but did not stop, Linux adoption and its ever increasing market share, especially in servers and small devices.

Freeze-the-market is an often used FUD technique. It involves pre-announcing a product or service. The pre-announced offering may be quite real or it may never actually become available (the latter is often called vaporware). Freeze-the-market works when the announcement is credible and the pre-announced offering raises concerns in the minds of decision makers that not waiting for it might be a serious mistake. It is used so frequently now that examples abound. The most skilled practitioners of freeze-the-market FUD actually do ultimately release the product or service, but often without some of its most FUD inspiring features. Consider the example of Microsoft's Windows Vista operating system. It was first slated for release in 2002 as the successor to Windows XP. After many embarrassing delays and a significant reduction in previously announced major new features, Vista finally began shipping in late 2006.

Using FUD is cheap, as in "talk is cheap." However, trying FUD and failing can be a bad sign when it has previously worked for you, as when IBM's failed "a better DOS than DOS, a better Windows than Windows" FUD campaign for OS/2 signaled the passing of the leadership baton from IBM to Microsoft and IBM's ultimate exit from the personal computer business entirely.

FUD can be effective in the short term but is difficult to sustain over a strategic time frame. Unless some of the concerns raised actually come true, the attacker can lose credibility, as Microsoft experienced with its anti-Linux campaign. The worst thing that can happen to the FUD purveyor is for the market to conclude that the emperor is naked. Unless handled with great skill, a strategic FUD attack can backfire and engender sympathy for the target company, resulting in exactly the opposite effect than was planned.

The Best Defense

How do you choose a defense against a strategic competitive threat from among a crown jewels attack and the various traditional competitive defenses? This is a tough business decision. There is no magic formula or decision tree to rely on. Sometimes the choice is to use several of these defenses in combination. Part two of this book provides a process to help with this decision making.

When there are viable crown jewels to target, you have staying power, and can handle the likely response to the attack, attacking the crown jewels has significant advantages that often make it the best strategic defense. A further look into the nuances of the crown jewels attack strategy, as represented by the four different styles of attack, is needed to understand and assess these advantages. Each of these styles has its own strengths and weaknesses. This is the subject of the next chapter.

4

Crown Jewels Attack Styles

"Alice: 'Would you tell me, please, which way I ought to go from here?' Cat: 'That depends a good deal on where you want to get to.'" – Lewis Carroll, Alice's Adventures in Wonderland

Attacking the crown jewels is not a one-size-fits-all strategy. This chapter defines the four styles that can be used for a crown jewels attack and how to select one. It also includes examples of attacks using each of the styles.

The two factors that determine attack style are growth opportunity and desire for control. Growth opportunity depends upon the extent to which can develop or enhance an offering that can make a significant future contribution to revenue and profit as part of the attack. Desire for control refers to the degree to which you want to control the attack. For maximum control, you need to own the attack weapon, the offering you intend to use against the competition. On the other hand, you may be willing to let someone else control the attack, and instead take the role of influencer, in which case you do not own the attack weapon. Both of these aspects of crown jewels attack style are further explored in this chapter.

Crown Jewels Attack

	No Growth	Growth	
Desire to Control ↑	Bamboozle Attack	Classic Attack	Own
	Jawbone Attack	Proxy Attack	Influence

Growth Opportunity →

Attack Style Quadrant
Copyright © 2007 Crown Jewels Group

Growth opportunity and desire for control form the two dimensions in the Attack Style Quadrant, and the choices made define the four crown jewels attack styles. These are the Classic Attack, the Proxy Attack, the Bamboozle Attack, and the Jawbone Attack.

Growth Opportunity

In addition to defending against a strategic competitive threat, attacking the crown jewels may give the company a product line that can make a significant future contribution to its revenue and profit. If consistent with overall strategy, always consider such an opportunity.

If the opportunity involves a new line of business, it may be one the company would not have pursued if it were not considering the attack. Adding the need to mount a strategic defense might tip the scales in favor of the opportunity. If you are going to commit resources to a crown jewels attack regardless, the incremental cost of entering the new market may make it much more appealing than it would be if judged exclusively on its own merits.

In the case of the Sony PlayStation threat to Microsoft Windows, the question for Bill Gates might have been framed as, "Do we want to use the need to mount a defense against PlayStation as an opportunity to enter the game console market?" The answer was that Microsoft wanted to enter this growth market.

Everyone wants growth, so why not always choose one of the growth styles? Growth does not come without risk and cost. The company must realistically decide if it is serious about the commitments, financial and otherwise, necessary to do two things. First, enhance, develop, or acquire the attack weapon. Second, market and support it.

The organization must be willing to do both with enough resources and tenacity over a sufficient period of time to produce significant revenue and profit. If the attack weapon does not fit the organization's current strategy, it needs to carefully consider if it is willing to adjust its overall strategy to encompass the new offering. If these enabling conditions are met, then consider one of the growth styles, the Classic Attack and the Proxy Attack. Otherwise, focus on the Bamboozle and Jawbone styles.

Desire For Control

In business, control is ultimately exerted by ownership. In the case of attacking the crown jewels, control of the attack is maximized by owning the product or service that will be used against your competitor, the attack weapon. The alternative to ownership is to influence another organization and let them own the attack weapon and control the attack. The control that comes with ownership increases your chances of success. It also involves a higher financial commitment. Owning the attack weapon may also be contrary to the overall strategy of the business.

This can be a cart-before-the-horse decision. Does the control or the ownership decision come first? The company's overall business strategy may make owning the attack weapon a clear choice, with the control it brings an outcome of ownership. Conversely, owning the attack weapon may be contrary to your business strategy. For example, you may be strictly a services company and the attack weapon may be a product, in which case you would not want to own it and thus must be willing to cede control. On the other hand, the nature of the threat may be such that you decide the company cannot afford the risk of giving up control of the attack and thus must own the attack weapon, perhaps changing its fundamental strategy to do so.

Returning to the Sony PlayStation threat to Microsoft Windows, the question for Bill Gates was, "Do we want to own the competing game console?" Gates probably reasoned that the attack needed the Microsoft brand in order to succeed. Besides, Microsoft always sought control of its offerings, especially strategic ones. Ownership was never seriously in question.

If the control/ownership decision is in favor of control, then consider the Classic and Bamboozle styles. Otherwise, focus on the Proxy and Jawbone styles.

The Classic Attack Style

In a classic attack, you have decided that you want to control the attack by owning the attack weapon, and want to use it as an opportunity to grow revenue and profit. While this attack style usually involves the greatest initial financial commitment of the four styles, ultimately you expect it to produce a source of ongoing profit. It also has the highest probability of succeeding, a consequence of control. This style is illustrated by Microsoft's Xbox attack against Sony's PlayStation.

A Classic Attack:
Why Microsoft Needs Xbox

Threat: Sony's PlayStation could evolve into a home PC replacement

Target: PlayStation as a game console

Weapon: Xbox

Objective: Divert Sony resources away from expanding the scope of PlayStation to defend it as a game console

Started: 1999

Success: High

This is the easiest initiative to explain to an organization and, once it gets rolling, the easiest one to focus on. Everyone can understand entering a growth market with a new offering. When the classic style is used, the rationale presented internally and externally is focused on the great opportunity the company has and how the initiative will take it and its customers to new heights of glory.

A Classic Attack:
Why Microsoft Needs Zune

In 2005, Microsoft had cause to worry about Apple's Macintosh for the first time in years. With less than 5% of worldwide personal computers, Apple presented no current threat to the Windows operating system monopoly. It actually helped Microsoft to have Apple in the personal computer market. Apple provided anti-trust cover for Microsoft by being such a well-known competitor. It also benefited Microsoft to have Apple try new things in the Macintosh operating system, OS X, that Microsoft could then adopt in Windows if they proved to be successful.

Macintosh was a closed system in which Apple controlled the basic computer hardware and operating system. If you wanted OS X, you had to buy a Macintosh computer from Apple. If you bought any other personal computer, you could not run OS X on it and it almost always came with Microsoft Windows already installed. Apple's computers did not even use the same type of computer processor as Windows computers. The two worlds were very separate.

Then Apple announced that it planned to use Intel processors in its computers. This is the same processor that most Windows personal computers use, and the rest use processors that are compatible with Intel's. Apple made it clear that OS X would be restricted to running on Macintosh computers. You still would not be able to run it on other personal computers.

A Classic Attack:
Why Microsoft Needs Zune

Threat: Apple's OS X could be freed to run on non-Apple PCs

Target: iPod/iTunes

Weapon: Zune

Objective: Divert Apple resources away from freeing OS X to defend iPod/iTunes

Started: 2006

Success: Too soon to tell, early signs positive

However, once OS X was ported to the Intel platform, Apple might at some point decide to support it on any Intel compatible personal computer, a relatively easy technical step, and sell it separately from the Macintosh hardware. This would bring OS X into head-to-head competition with Windows. It could be a very successful competitor and gain substantial market share fast. This would not be a good development for Microsoft.

Defense of Windows is a primary Microsoft strategic imperative, and Microsoft wanted to keep OS X pinned down on Apple hardware to keep it marginalized. As Apple's switch to Intel processors moved forward, Microsoft targeted Apple's crown jewels, iPod and iTunes, with a directly competing product line called Zune, announced in 2006. By doing so, it expected Apple to vigorously defend iPod and iTunes. This would divert resources that might otherwise go towards unleashing OS X against Windows, resulting in a classic style crown jewels attack.

This was not the first attack Microsoft had made against iPod and iTunes. In 2004, Microsoft launched a logo and testing initiative called PlaysForSure. This was intended to assure customers that PlaysForSure music and video content would work on PlaysForSure devices, and bring order out of the chaos of competing digital rights management schemes and player technologies that befuddled them. Windows Media Player would be the hub, connecting PlaysForSure content with PlaysForSure devices. Hardware and content vendors climbed on board, including BestBuy, Gateway, Napster, Samsung, Linksys, Audiovox, Virgin Electronics, Wal-Mart, Dell, and HP.

It took the various vendors a long time to get all the pieces of the puzzle to line up properly. Before the Plays-ForSure ecosystem had a decent number of devices and a good supply of content working together smoothly, Apple's iPod and iTunes had captured seventy percent of the market. A key to Apple's iPod success was iTunes. Unlike Microsoft's Media Player that ran only on Windows, free iTunes software ran on Windows and Macintosh computers. Where Microsoft had to count on myriad vendors to all get PlaysForSure right, Apple controlled all the parts of the system, from the iTunes content store to the iPod players, and thus could assure they all worked together seamlessly.

When Apple announced in 2005 that it would switch to Intel microprocessors, Microsoft decided it had to change attacks. Mimicking its Xbox attack against Sony, and learning the lesson of this marketplace from Apple's successes and PlaysForSure's difficulties, Microsoft cloned the iPod/iTunes model and announced Zune, leaving its PlaysForSure partners in the lurch. The Zune device looks like an iPod. Content comes from an online store called Zune Marketplace, which is like the iTunes store. Zune software running on Windows glues it all together, as the iTunes software does for iPods and the iTunes store.

In its PlaysForSure-to-Zune attack evolution, Microsoft followed a common pattern. It increased its control of the attack weapon. With the PlaysForSure weapon, Microsoft relied on many partners to make the attack successful. Not so with Zune. The lesson here is that when an attack does not work as desired, consider increasing control of the attack weapon. Sometimes this means developing a completely new weapon.

Apple was vulnerable to this Microsoft strategy. It had become hooked on the fat margins Macintosh provided and this kept it from truly competing with Windows by setting OS X free. Regardless of all the marketing hype about Macintosh and OS X, computers were not much of a growth story for Apple. The iPod/iTunes empire was. For Apple, it was iPod/iTunes that must be defended at all costs. With Microsoft attacking Apple's crown jewels this way, it was unlikely that Apple would devote the resources needed to plan and implement a generic OS X versus Windows strategy, even if it found the will to do so.

The iPod/iTunes market is appealing to Microsoft. It has high growth potential. The PlaysForSure problems convinced Microsoft that no one else would emerge as a serious competitor to Apple that could be used as a proxy. So Microsoft chose to directly enter this market with Zune, with the intention of being a dominant player itself in the long run. Microsoft has stated and demonstrated that it is willing to invest in a new venture over many years before it becomes profitable. This is especially true when doing so is essential to the defense of Windows or Office. Microsoft has staying power, huge resources, and has demonstrated strategic focus and discipline, with a very long attention span.

A Classic Attack:
Oracle Versus SAP

In the 1990s, SAP was the dominant enterprise business application software company. Most SAP customer installations used Oracle's market leading database product as the database engine for the SAP software. Meanwhile, Oracle had entered the enterprise business application market, though its offerings there were second rate and it was an also-ran.

In 1998, rumors were rampant that SAP was looking for its own database software so that it could stop being a source of revenue to its erstwhile competitor. The rumors centered around Sybase and Informix, two of Oracle's long-time major database competitors that Oracle had finally beaten into second-tier status after many years of brutal, head-to-head competition. Oracle had long been concerned about the potential threat posed by SAP if it entered the database market, and these rumors triggered an attacking the crown jewels defense. CEO Larry Ellison took direct control of managing the tepid business applications product line. Ellison was determined to build this line of business into a world-class competitor for SAP. He was soon publicly stating that SAP was Oracle's number one target. Defending against this Oracle attack would divert SAP resources away from any database offering of its own.

A Classic Attack:
Oracle vs. SAP

Threat: An SAP database product could threaten Oracle's database products

Target: SAP business applications

Weapon: Oracle business applications

Objective: Divert SAP resources away from a database product to defend its business applications

Started: 1998

Success: High

At the time, Oracle's business application product line was an uninspiring, loose collection of weak applications that the sales force could not effectively sell. Two years after Ellison took the helm, a re-architected suite of business applications was released to the market. With over 5,000 known bugs, it was an embarrassing disaster. Ellison had used the "compile-ship-debug" approach that he had used 20 years before in the early days of Oracle's database business. There followed a couple of years of frantic debugging while customers fumed.

Then Oracle, which had largely gotten to be database king by growing organically and eschewing major acquisitions, boldly made an aggressive offer to acquire business applications rival PeopleSoft. In the aftermath of the dot-com bust, the price was right. When the Justice Department lost its antitrust action to block the deal, the way was paved for an acquisition spree. Ellison announced that Oracle intended to consolidate the business applications market. He scooped up over twenty companies and turned the enterprise business applications market into a two horse race, Oracle versus SAP. Oracle executed the complex integration of its acquisitions superbly. By 2006, its enterprise business applications product line had achieved several strong quarters in a row, and the market had become pretty much an Oracle and SAP duopoly.

How did SAP respond to this unrelenting attack? They attacked back. This reaction is described in detail later in this chapter as an example of a proxy attack. The bottom line, however, is that after some twists and turns, by 2006 SAP had clearly lost interest in competing in the database market. Oracle's classic crown jewels attack had succeeded.

The Proxy Attack Style

In a proxy attack, you want to use the growth opportunity presented by the attack weapon's market. However, you either do not want or do not need to control the attack weapon by owning it. Like the classic attack, this style usually involves a major initial financial commitment and the ultimate expectation of ongoing profits, but without the comfort of control.

In a proxy attack, lack of ownership means that you must rely on another organization, the proxy, to own and control the attack weapon. Your role becomes one of supporting the proxy organization to make the attack weapon successful, and doing so in a manner that adds a significant revenue stream to your business. This is done by providing products and/or services that are part of the attack weapon's support ecosystem. Thus, the success of your support offerings depends on the success of the proxy and its attack weapon. You and the proxy are, as they say, joined at the hip.

The rise of the open-source movement has made software industry proxy attacks more frequent and appealing than they had been previously. In open source, the company that develops the product relies heavily on a network of volunteers for product development. The software source code is freely available, and the software itself is free and can be distributed without charge, but all modifications and distributions must be similarly open and free. Making money in open source comes from selling support, documentation and training, and from selling other products that use one or more free open-source products. For example, many companies sell server-based products that include the free open-source Linux operating system, Apache web server, and MySQL database software.

Prior to open source, finding a suitable software proxy was difficult. Often this meant funding another company, sometime a start-up, to influence it enough to execute the attack. With open-source increasing in popularity and respect, new proxy options are available. You can join an existing open-source effort that has the attack weapon you need, like IBM did with Linux. You can also seed an open-source project with an attack weapon by donating an existing proprietary software product, like SAP did with SAP/DB, donating it to MySQL, which then renamed it MaxDB. In either case, you exert influence by heavily supporting the open-source product, especially by assigning your paid staff to the development effort. Both of these examples are detailed later in this chapter.

Since you influence the proxy but do not control it, a proxy attack is harder to manage than a classic attack and thus less likely to succeed. It is not unusual for a proxy attack to ultimately turn into a classic attack when attack success appears to require the control of ownership.

A Proxy Attack:
Why IBM Loves Linux

During the 1990s, as Microsoft grew into a software mega-giant, IBM recognized it as a strategic threat. IBM was determined to keep Microsoft from becoming a more effective competitor to its core strategic business, complex enterprise technology solutions. To contain Microsoft, IBM attacked one of Microsoft's crown jewels, its Windows operating system. Keeping Microsoft pinned down defending Windows would cause it to use resources that might otherwise go into competing more effectively in the complex enterprise technology solutions market. While IBM competed with Microsoft on many fronts, like the Notes versus Exchange competition, it needed a focused strategic attack on Windows.

A Proxy Attack:
Why IBM Loves Linux

Threat:	Microsoft could get very good at complex enterprise technology solutions
Target:	Microsoft Windows
Weapon:	Linux
Objective:	Divert Microsoft resources away from complex enterprise technology solutions to defend Windows
Started:	1998
Success:	High

IBM's OS/2 debacle was the first attempt at this. OS/2 started in the 1980s as a joint Microsoft-IBM effort to replace the DOS operating system with a multi-tasking, graphical operating system. At that time, Microsoft Windows was clunky and struggling. But by 1990, OS/2 was owned solely by IBM after the joint development relationship it had with Microsoft collapsed, and a vastly improved

Windows was dominating the market. OS/2 gave IBM a weapon with which to attack Windows, and it did so vigorously, led by the slogan "a better DOS than DOS, a better Windows than Windows." But Microsoft Windows crushed OS/2 in the market. This defeat led IBM to realize that it did not really want to be in the personal computer operating system market and it let OS/2 die. Ultimately, IBM decided it did not really like being in the personal computer market at all, and it sold its personal computer manufacturing business to Lenovo in 2005.

IBM's next attempt at attacking Windows was much more sophisticated. IBM decided to get another company to act as its proxy and mount the attack on Windows. IBM would assure the proxy had staying power and the resources, focus, and will to launch an effective, sustained attack. How did IBM do this? IBM fell in love with the open-source operating system, Linux. IBM jumped aboard the Linux bandwagon, arguably assuring Linux its current level of success through its direct and indirect support.

IBM has worked hard to become a good citizen in the open-source community, no easy transition for a company that had built its might selling products and services based on its well protected intellectual property. It had spent an estimated $1 billion through 2006 on Linux development and marketing. IBM provides direct resources to the open-source Linux project. It advocates for Linux and the open-source model. It provides a vast array of Linux-specific services. It uses Linux whenever possible in its solutions. It partners with other members of the Linux ecosystem. It is an effective advocate for open-source initiatives by government agencies and other organizations worldwide, and backs its advocacy with services to help those initiatives succeed.

By 2006, the outcome of this attack was stunning. Linux was giving Microsoft fits competing with Windows on the server side and in small devices. The Microsoft brain trust was haunted by the prospect of someone coming along with the right formula for wrapping the necessary software and services around Linux to make it a true Windows desktop competitor. Strategic adoption of Linux by many governmental agencies around the world, often supported or instigated by IBM, appeared to guarantee a long-term Windows-Linux duopoly. And the success of Linux had spurred on all sorts of other open-source efforts across the spectrum of Microsoft's product lines, broadening the threat beyond Windows. IBM's proxy attack against Windows with Linux had vastly reduced Microsoft's commitment of resources in the complex enterprise technology solutions market.

A Proxy Attack: SAP Versus Oracle

This example illustrates two companies engaging in reciprocal use of the crown jewels attack strategy. One worked, the other failed. The attack that worked was Oracle's classic attack against the potential threat that enterprise business application giant SAP would enter the database business, as described earlier in this chapter. The attack that failed was SAP's short-lived attempt to turn that potential threat into an actual one, attacking Oracle's market leading database product line. This attack started as a classic attack, then changed into a proxy attack.

A Proxy Attack:
SAP vs. Oracle

Threat: Oracle business applications directly threaten SAP business applications

Target: Oracle database products

Weapon: Adabas D to SAP/DB to MaxDB

Objective: Divert Oracle resources away from business applications to defend Oracle's database products

Started: 1999

Success: Failed

In 1999, business applications software giant SAP acquired all rights to a database product called Adabas D from a company named Software AG, and renamed it SAP/DB. For SAP, Adabas D had one particularly appealing feature, its Oracle compatibility mode. SAP now had the attack weapon it needed to launch a classic crown jewels defense against the strategic threat posed by Oracle in its competition in the enterprise business applications market. SAP attacked Oracle's crown jewels, its database product line. The outcome of this attack, if successful, would be to divert resources away from Oracle's business applications efforts. In 2000, SAP converted proprietary SAP/DB to open-source, with the idea of offering it free with its business applications, except for support costs, but it retained ownership of the open-source project.

Under relentless competitive attack in its core enterprise business applications market from the likes of Oracle, PeopleSoft, Seibel Systems, and others, SAP refocused its resources on defending that offering. It decided it did not want the level of commitment that came with owning the database product attack weapon it had acquired. By 2003, SAP had turned SAP/DB over to open-source database vendor MySQL, and it was renamed once more, this time as MaxDB. MySQL positioned MaxDB as its high-end enterprise database offering. SAP continued to support MaxDB in a variety of ways, including providing a team of programmers for the open-source project, but had ceded ownership.

Before long, SAP found it did not have the tenacity and focus necessary to sustain its proxy attack and commit fully to having a truly competitive offering in the database market, regardless of ownership. MaxDB did not gain appreciable market share and the attack on Oracle was a failure.

The Bamboozle Attack Style

A bamboozle attack is used when you want to own the attack weapon but do not see much revenue potential for your company in its market, usually because the attack weapon does not fit your overall business strategy and model. The idea is to have a lightweight offering that costs you relatively little to keep alive, and that threatens to become a heavyweight competitive threat but never quite gets there.

A bamboozle attack is primarily a marketing activity. For a bamboozle attack to succeed, you must confuse your competitor about your future intentions and make them take the attack seriously because of what it might become, rather than what it actually is. Bamboozle attacks often rely on enthralling industry analysts and pundits with the potential you have to do something wonderful should you ever seriously enter the market. They then become your propaganda squad. It often helps to coyly deny that you intend to compete with your target, all the while making small moves that could be interpreted as heading in that direction. Bamboozle attacks are smoke-and-mirrors ploys, cheered along by a bewitched audience. As in the Wizard of Oz, there is less behind the curtain than you are led to believe.

Bamboozle attacks can evolve into classic or proxy attacks. Sometimes the bamboozler discovers serious revenue potential in the attack weapon and decides to make a full commitment to the market, a classic attack. In other cases, the bamboozler sees an opportunity to spin off or sell the attack weapon to new owners that they are convinced they can influence to continue the attack for them as a proxy attack.

A Bamboozle Attack:
The Google Office Bamboozle

Google is in the business of monitizing search through advertising. They therefore must strategically defend their search dominance. Microsoft represents one of Google's biggest strategic threats because, while it lags behind Google and Yahoo in search, it is committed to search as a category and is using its proven approach of continuous improvement to endeavor to slowly, inexorably become a better and better competitor. Microsoft is relentless, focused, and has the resources to keep at this for as long as it takes.

Meanwhile, Google launched a bamboozle attack on one of Microsoft's crown jewels, Microsoft Office. Google does not seem to want to actually compete directly with Office. There is not a clean fit between a full-featured business suite of personal productivity products and Google's "monetize search through advertising" model. A well executed bamboozle attack, however, gives Google control yet requires little investment. Since Microsoft has two overarching strategic imperatives, defend Windows and defend Office, a successful perceived threat to Office would inevitably force Microsoft to shore it up, using resources that might otherwise go to improving search.

To start the attack, in 2004 Google began developing or acquiring bits and pieces that seemed like they could be assembled into a Microsoft Office competitor. By mid-2005, they had email, a calendar, a spreadsheet, a word processor, and a few other odds and ends, and were ready to bamboozle.

A Bamboozle Attack:
The Google Office Bamboozle

Threat: Microsoft's search offerings threaten Google's search offerings

Target: Microsoft Office

Weapon: A possible Google Office offering

Objective: Divert Microsoft resources away from search to defend Office

Started: 2004

Success: High

All of the Google components were lightweight compared to the rich feature and function sets in Office's components. No matter. Google has a mystifying affect on the media and analysts. Google seems to be nimble, hip, and leading-edge, where Microsoft appears sluggish, stuffy, and stuck in the 20th century. Google products are, for the most part, free to users. Google is all about cool technologies with esoteric names like AJAX and Web 2.0, and has a gigantic price-earnings ratio. Microsoft seems mired in dependence on upgrade revenue, stodgy technology, antitrust actions, and a stagnant stock price. This Google mystique enables the bamboozle. Every Google move, no matter how trivial, is met with great media and analyst fanfare and breathless speculation on what it all means, especially to Microsoft. As Bill Gates lamented, "If it was rumored they [Google] were doing pizza, you'd think it was going to be zero calories and free."

Google kept nudging its Office threat along. In August of 2005, it assembled the awkwardly named Google Apps for Your Domain suite that bundled Google Mail, Google Talk, Google Calendar, and Google Page Creator into a suite of online applications that can be added to a web domain. The base offering was free, aimed at small and medium-sized organizations. Then in 2006, Google bundled its Writely word processor with Google Spreadsheets into a free service called Google Docs and Spreadsheets. Predictably, the press and analysts went gaga over each of these meager actions. Meanwhile, Google denied that these were steps towards a Google Office offering. No matter. The denials merely served to fuel the frenzy of speculation. Google has even become a sort of spiritual leader to a group of emerging companies working on their own Office component replacements in what has become known as the Office 2.0 initiative.

This threat to Microsoft Office became one of Microsoft's architect-in-chief Ray Ozzie's top priorities. Ozzie, a computer industry legend, succeeded Bill Gates in the chief architect role and was hired in 2005 in large part to combat Google and move Microsoft into the 21st century. The first Microsoft response was in 2006. Called Microsoft Office Live, it turned out to be more of an "Office Small." Rather than an online suite of Office-like productivity tools, Office Live consisted of a set of online services including email, web hosting, and contact management, targeted at small businesses. This confusing branding fooled no one.

A bamboozled Microsoft continues to search for a good response to the elusive Google Office threat that does not cannibalize its billions of dollars of annual Office revenue. This quest diverts resources that could otherwise be used in its search efforts. Google, meanwhile, focuses resources almost exclusively on its mainstay fast-growth opportunity, increasing the breadth, depth, and use of its search machine and further extending its advertising model.

A Bamboozle Attack: Amazon Versus eBay

In 1998, Amazon.com and eBay dominated the fledgling but rapidly growing online commerce market. Both had grown from 1995 start-ups to dominate two different parts of what was then called the "new economy." Amazon was the online superstore, offering fixed-price brand-name merchandise. The eBay model was more like a worldwide garage sale, where folks offered their merchandise, often used, in online auctions.

Under CEO Jeff Bezos, Amazon had invested heavily in infrastructure. It had built a massive high-volume, high-performance online store, with careful attention to all the user experience details from finding merchandise to loading it into an electronic shopping cart to effortless checkout. Amazon had also constructed a network of high-tech warehouses capable of rapidly, accurately, and seamlessly fulfilling orders. Bezos had an expansive vision for Amazon that included not only being the premier online superstore, but also providing the online commerce infra-structure to other merchants, including competitors.

A Bamboozle Attack:
Amazon vs. eBay

Threat: eBay could expand its support for fixed-price, brand-name manufacturers and merchants

Target: eBay's auction market

Weapon: Amazon's auction offering

Objective: Divert eBay resources away from offerings for fixed-price, brand-name sellers to defend its auction offerings

Started: 1999

Success: High

During the same period, eBay had taken a different path. It warehoused and shipped no merchandise. Instead, eBay functioned as an auction broker between sellers and customers searching for a bargain. It too invested heavily in online commerce infrastructure, building a powerful auction site. Around the world, people with something to sell, however odd, could find people interested in buying for the right price, and vice-versa.

Amazon saw eBay as a potential strategic competitive threat. The threat was that eBay could build on its infor-mation technology infrastructure to facilitate online com-merce for large, fixed price merchants. Without the overhead of warehousing and distributing merchandise, eBay could leverage capital more efficiently than Amazon. This was always the weak link in the Amazon vision, and Bezos foresaw many more years of heavy capital investment with problematic profitability. The threat he feared was that eBay could offer a potentially more capital efficient online model for large, brand-name, fixed-price merchants.

Because Amazon sold fixed-price merchandise and eBay used an auction system, the battle between the two was generally characterized by observers as a dual between the fixed-price and auction models. Amazon, however, was not overly concerned about eBay adding a fixed-price capability. Amazon was much more concerned about eBay's seller community. Amazon wanted to curtail eBay's seller appeal to fixed-price, brand-name manufacturers and merchants. They were Amazon's target sellers. From Amazon's perspective, eBay was welcome to serve the used-merchandise, odd-lot, and small sellers.

To keep eBay in its niche, Amazon launched a bamboozle attack. A crash three-month project duplicated eBay functionality built over Amazon's existing infrastructure, and in March of 1999, Amazon launched its own auction site. This was the attack weapon for an unambiguous attack against eBay's crown jewels. A few weeks later, Amazon acquired the auction site LiveBid.com, a company eBay had been courting, heightening Amazon's apparent threat to eBay.

Amazon kept moving this effort forward, but did not really commit to an all-out attempt to win in the auction model market. However, Amazon's capability to, at any time, focus more resources on improving and marketing its auction business would keep eBay concerned. All Amazon needed to do was make occasional enhancements to the auction site and feed the business media fuel to keep reporting on the Amazon-eBay contest as an auction versus fixed-price battle. Let the outside world think that this was what concerned Amazon. If this diverted eBay resources away from creating an effective online commerce alternative for Amazon's fixed-price, brand-name sellers, then the bamboozle would be successful.

CEO Meg Whitman led eBay's reaction to the Amazon attack in several ways. She focused on acquiring other auction sites to increase the breadth and depth of eBay's bazaar. She began adding fixed-price capability to eBay's model, but for its existing seller community. She also accelerated rolling out new and improved infrastructure capabilities, focused on the existing eBay buyer and seller community profile. What eBay did not do was expand much in the direction Amazon feared. Its resources were otherwise occupied defending against the potential threat posed by the Amazon bamboozle attack.

Amazon has continued to successfully bamboozle eBay by fiddling with its auction offering. Each time it does, it gets the requisite publicity and buzz going about the threat it poses to eBay. This, despite having less than 1% of the online auction market to eBay's 95% in 2006.

The Jawbone Attack Style

What do you do when you neither want to control the attack weapon nor seek growth from its market? You try to talk someone else into doing both for you. Clearly, this presents significant challenges. You must be very persuasive but, unlike a proxy attack, you can afford to offer little tangible support.

This jawboning is usually very public, often led by the company's CEO and trumpeted by his minions. The surface message is typically about something that is urgently needed and will benefit the world if only someone (else) would step up to the challenge. The underlying message, to paraphrase King Henry II, is "Who will rid me of this meddlesome competitor?"

To induce others to mount the desired attack, the company leading the jawboning often has to "put its money where its mouth is" and do what amounts to a demonstration project to jump start the attack weapon market or at least nudge it in the desired direction. The jawboning company has no intention of actually getting into the market, as it usually makes quite clear, and often drops the project as soon as possible. This proof-of-concept is frequently done under the cover of a subsidiary company or an internal research laboratory.

A jawbone attack is similar to a FUD attack and they are often used together. Like FUD, a jawbone attack can be effective in the short term but is difficult to sustain over a strategic time frame. Unless someone else steps forward to actually mount the desired attack with a sustained and credible effort, the jawboners ultimately lose credibility.

A jawbone attack is unlikely to succeed. Use it only as a last resort or as a short-term prelude to another defensive strategy. Most jawbone attacks either die because the target competitors do not take them seriously, or they are changed to one of the other three styles after jawboning fails. Whenever possible, avoid using the jawbone attack by making an affirmative choice to use an attack weapon that either provides you with a growth opportunity or that you are willing to control, or both. Recognize that if you choose a jawbone attack against a truly strategic threat, you are probably putting off making a more committed decision rather than defending your strategy against the competitive threat.

A Jawbone Attack: Oracle Versus Microsoft

In 1995, Microsoft released SQL Server 6.0, a major rewrite of its database product. While previous releases had been developed jointly with database software company Sybase and were based on Sybase technology, this new release was solely a Microsoft effort. It featured vastly improved performance, scalability, reliability, and management features aimed directly at corporate database administrators.

Database giant Oracle was at this time a one-trick pony. That pony was its database product line. This had to be defended at all costs. Oracle had up to then succeeded in positioning SQL Server as a low-end solution for lightweight applications. Larry Ellison, Oracle's CEO, knew that this FUD defense was not going to work now that SQL Server could deliver the goods. Microsoft's marketing machine finally had the competitive product it needed to effectively combat Oracle.

A Jawbone Attack: Oracle vs. Microsoft	
Threat:	SQL Server threatens Oracle's database products
Target:	Wintel PCs
Weapon:	Network Computer (NC)
Objective:	Divert Microsoft resources away from SQL Server to defend the Wintel PC platform
Started:	1995
Success:	Failed

Oracle was a classic enterprise software company. Ellison had no desire to go head-to-head with any other Microsoft products. What Oracle did do was launch a jawbone attack. Oracle attacked the very notion of a personal computer that needed a heavyweight operating system, and thus threatened Microsoft's crown jewels, its Windows operating system. Should such an attack take hold, Microsoft would certainly defend its crown jewels, and in the process divert resources away from SQL Server.

The attack weapon was the Network Computer (NC). Oracle's jawboner-in-chief, Larry Ellison, launched the attack in a 1995 speech. His message was straightforward: personal computers had become too complicated and expensive. NCs would be simpler, less expensive devices connected to the Internet. Most of the software and data would be stored on servers. Software would be based on Sun Microsystems' Java, thus extending the threat to all Microsoft software. Of course, all data would be in Oracle databases, which would ultimately replace the file system.

The jawbone attack had an initial bandwagon effect. It rode the wave of Internet hype, floating on the surface of the ever expanding dot-com bubble. Respectable business publications like *BusinessWeek* and *The Economist* wrote breathless articles predicting the demise of PCs and the rise of NCs. Numerous computer industry pundits and leaders, like Sun Microsystems CEO Scott McNealy, added their voices to Ellison's in a growing chorus of pro-NC, anti-PC propaganda.

Oracle commissioned the development of a specification for NCs that others could freely use. Companies like IBM, Sun, and a few small fry built NC devices. The market yawned in disinterest. Oracle then even set up a subsidiary, Network Computer, Inc., to develop software for NCs. Thus the jawbone attack seemed on its way to becoming a proxy or classic attack. Still, NCs got no market traction.

This occurred for several reasons. Competition in the personal computer industry led to cheaper, easier to use PCs. The rise of the web browser and the example of the Macintosh led Microsoft to improve ease-of-use across its software product lines. Handheld electronic gadgets with web capabilities became the true network appliances, with extreme ease of use and very low price points. Thus the two NC differentiators, cost and ease of use, were neutralized.

The network computer jawbone attack failed. Microsoft carefully monitored NC developments, but the threat never reached the threshold necessary to appreciably impact how it allocated its resources. It did not slow Microsoft's development and marketing of SQL Server. SQL Server has continued to gain market share and has established itself as a very significant competitor for Oracle in the database market.

Attack Style Comparisons

The characteristics of each of the four crown jewels attack styles are determined by the desire for control and growth opportunity factors in the Attack Style Quadrant. For example, each of the four styles presents its own challenges, as follows:

- The main challenge for a classic attack is the initial investment.

- The main challenges for a proxy attack are finding a suitable proxy and keeping the attack on target without control.

- The main challenges for a bamboozle attack are convincing the competitor to take the attack seriously and sustaining the effort with little revenue expectation.

- The main challenge for a jawbone attack is convincing the competitor to take the attack seriously.

Each of the four attack styles also has its own characteristic relative potential cost and financial contribution, as well as potential for strategic success. These are summarized and compared in the chart along with the typical evolutionary path each style tends to take.

	Potential Cost	Potential Contribution	Potential Success	Typical Evolution
Classic Attack	High	High	High	
Proxy Attack	Moderate	High	High	Classic
Bamboozle Attack	Moderate	Low	Moderate	Classic Proxy
Jawbone Attack	Low	Low	Low	Classic Proxy Bamboozle

Do not rely on these characteristics to choose an attack style. Instead, use them to plan ahead for the likely consequences of the choices made in the Attack Style Quadrant. Part two of this book presents a detailed, step-by-step process for identifying and evaluating competitive threats and then choosing appropriate defenses. The choice of a defense is based on strategic fit, net cost, and chance of success. This is examined in depth as part of the methodology discussion.

Part 2

Strategic Competitive Defense Planning

"Let our advance worrying become advance thinking and planning." – Winston Churchill

5

The Planning Process

"In preparing for battle I have always found that plans are useless, but planning is indispensable."
– Dwight Eisenhower

A strategic defense is a serious undertaking. To be successful, it must be a full-fledged strategic initiative. Any organization, no matter how large or how wealthy, can handle only a limited number of such endeavors without becoming defocused, scattered, and confused. You are committing the organization to a critical, major course of action that you intend to follow for a long period of time. If you change course and abort the initiative without a compelling reason, the organization may lose confidence in its leadership's ability to chart a wise course and stick to it. It is therefore essential to focus on a limited number of strategic initiatives. This means reserving crown jewels attacks and the other strategic competitive defenses for truly strategic threats.

The Strategic Competitive Defense Planning Process

Step 1: List Competitive Threats

Step 2: Evaluate Competitive Threats

Step 3: Select Candidate Crown Jewels To Target

Step 4: Develop Prototype Attacks

Step 5: Evaluate Prototype Attacks

Step 6: Consider Other Defenses

Step 7: Plan, Decide, Implement

This chapter spells out a process for assessing strategic competitive threats, selecting the ones to focus on, and planning defenses against them. This planning is often done as part of an organization's overall strategic planning process. While there are many comprehensive approaches to strategic planning that may be used, they all include threat analysis, with competitive threats as one of the types considered. The process presented in this chapter can replace or augment that part of your strategic planning process. The strategic competitive defense planning process can also be used as a stand-alone activity. Whether used as part of a larger process or by itself, make this an annual activity led, though not necessarily facilitated, by the CEO.

There are several worksheets used in this process that are grouped together in the next few pages. Copies of these worksheets can be downloaded from the following website:

www.AttackingTheCrownJewels.com

After the worksheets, the rest of this chapter elaborates on each of the steps in the process. Then the next chapter illustrates the process with a fictional case study that includes examples of completed worksheets.

Threat Evaluation Worksheet Steps 1 and 2			
Threat Statement	Severe (1–5)	Robust (1–5)	Credible (1–5)

**Strategic Competitor Profile Worksheet
Step 2**

Competitor:

Mission Statement:

Key Strengths:

Key Weaknesses:

Revenue Sources:

Other Information:

102 Attacking The Crown Jewels

Candidate Attack Target Worksheet Step 3	
Threat Statement	**Crown Jewels Target**

Strategic Defense Worksheet Steps 4, 5 and 6	
Threat Statement:	
Attack Statement:	
Strategic Fit (1-5):	**Chance Of Success: (1-5):**
Net Cost:	
Additional Defenses:	
Likely Response:	

Competitive Defense Alternatives Worksheet Step 7			
Threat Statement:			
	Strategic Fit / **Chance Of Success**	**Net Cost**	**Rank**
Alternative 1:			
Likely Response 1:			
Alternative 2:			
Likely Response 2:			
Alternative 3:			
Likely Response 3:			
Alternative 4:			
Likely Response 4:			

Step 1:
List Competitive Threats

The objective of this step is to cast a wide net and develop an extensive list of competitive threats. This has many of the characteristics of a brainstorming activity. At this stage, the more threats listed, the better. It is therefore important to avoid filtering out any ideas. Avoid competitive self-delusion. You will get to prune this list later in the process.

In this step, you are looking for specific strategic threats from specific companies. To develop this list, brainstorm the following questions:

- What are the existing threats from current competitors?

- What actions might our current competitors take that could cause new threats?

- What actions might our current partners take that could cause them to become threats?

- What actions might companies in adjacent markets to ours take that could cause new threats?

- Are any of our customers likely to become competitors?

- What are possible substitutes for our products and services?

- Who are potential new entrants into our markets?

- What emerging technologies may be used to create competition for us?

Competitive Threat Statement Formats

[competitor]'s *[existing product or service]* is a threat to *[your product or service]*

- or -

[competitor]'s *[existing product or service]* is a threat to *[your product or service]* if *[how it might evolve]*

- or -

[competitor]'s possible *[product or service]* is a potential threat to *[your product or service]*

List each threat on the Threat Evaluation Worksheet in the form of a competitive threat statement. A competitive threat statement has one of the formats shown above.

The following are examples of threat statements that might be used by some well-known companies against some well-known competitors:

Competitive Threat Statement
Examples

Google: Yahoo's advertising-financed search engine is a threat to our advertising-financed search engine

Microsoft: Sony's PlayStation is a threat to Windows if it evolves into a home computer replacement

Oracle: SAP's possible database product is a potential threat to our database product

---

The next step is to evaluate each competitive threat statement.

Step 2:
Evaluate Competitive Threats

The objective in step one was to produce an exhaustive list of possible threats. Now it is time to reduce the size of the list by rating each competitive threat statement for severity, robustness and credibility.

Step 2-a: Competitor Profile

Before rating a threat, it is useful to develop a brief strategic profile of the competitor using the Strategic Competitor Profile Worksheet. There are many sources of this competitive intelligence, and a little time spent with a web search engine can produce gratifying results.

The following are suggestions for completing the Competitor Profile Worksheet.

Mission Statement

A mission statement should, directly or indirectly, communicate three essential ideas:

- What the organization does

- Who it does it for

- How it does it differently from others

This can usually be done in no more than three sentences. You can often find an organization's mission statement on its web site. If it is useful, by all means use it. You may, however, want to develop your own view of its mission, especially if the mission statement it uses is too vague and all-encompassing for your purposes.

Here is an example. This is Google's mission statement as of 2006, quoted from their web site: "Google's mission is to organize the world's information and make it universally accessible and useful." It says what they do, though at a pretty abstract level. It implies both who they do it for and how they do it that is special. Now here is how a competitor doing strategic planning with a three to five year planning horizon might rewrite Google's mission: "Google provides the fastest, most useful, and easiest-to-use web search results for anyone with Internet access. They monetize web search through advertising targeted to search results. They provide Internet users with free or low cost web based services that leverage their computing infrastructure and provide them with opportunities to extend the reach of search and targeted advertising."

Key Strengths

Consider the following questions to determine the competitor's key strengths:

- What do they do better than most competitors?

- What resources do they have that give them an advantage over most competitors?

- What assets do they have that give them an advantage over most competitors?

- What other advantages, tangible and intangible, do they have over most competitors?

If you believe a key strength is likely to change, make a note of that and the reasons for your expectation.

Some examples of areas that can be key strengths are workforce skills, intellectual property, technology infrastructure, branding, production capacity, distribution capability, partnerships, economies of scale, access to natural resources, supplier relationships, customer loyalty, quality, finances, and management.

Key Weaknesses

Consider the following questions to determine the competitor's key weaknesses:

- What do they do less well than most competitors?

- What resources do they lack that put them at a disadvantage compared to most competitors?

- What assets do they lack that put them at a disadvantage compared to most competitors?

- What other disadvantages, tangible and intangible, do they have compared to most competitors?

If you believe a key weakness is likely to change, make a note of that and the reasons for your expectation.

Weaknesses can occur in the same areas as strengths, including workforce skills, intellectual property, technology infrastructure, branding, production capacity, distribution capability, partnerships, economies of scale, access to natural resources, supplier relationships, customer loyalty, quality, finances and management.

Revenue Sources

Estimate the organization's revenue and margins by product line. Also assess the trends for revenue and profitability by product lines. Attempt to get enough detail to answer the following questions:

- Which product lines are growing revenue, and is the growth rate high, medium, or low?

- Which product lines have shrinking revenue, and is the rate of contraction high, medium, or low?

- Which product lines are growing in profitability, and is the growth rate high, medium, or low?

- Which product lines have shrinking profitability, and is the rate of contraction high, medium, or low?

A strategic revenue source is one that is expected to make a significant contribution to future profit and/or revenue for a particular strategic planning horizon. Thus, a current source of revenue that is expected to grow may make a small contribution in the present but be very important strategically. On the other hand, a product line may provide a large amount of profit and/or revenue currently but be in decline and not expected to make an important contribution strategically. The answers to the above questions help determine the extent to which a competitor's product line is strategic. This characterization will be used to help assess threat credibility and select their crown jewels to attack.

Other Information

Use this section of the form to document other items that you believe help you evaluate how the competitor is likely to behave in the market. This information may include things like ownership, key executive profiles and turnover, recent P&L and balance sheet data and trends, tendency to grow organically or by acquisition, pricing policies, marketing methods, target customer segments, geographical locations, and number and location of employees.

Attachments may be necessary, but brevity is essential so that you do not get buried in detail. Focus on information that enhances your ability to put yourself in the competitor CEO's shoes and predict the competitor's future actions.

Step 2-b: Rate The Threat

With the competitor's profile as background information, rate each competitive threat statement for severity, robustness, and credibility.

Is The Threat Severe?

To determine if a threat is severe, ask this question: would the threat, if realized, prevent you from reaching your big-picture objectives with a three to five year horizon? These objectives are usually stated in terms of revenue, profit, and market-share, but you may come up with others that are subject to competitive threat.

While this may seem like simply a yes-or-no decision, in practice these judgments are not quite so absolute. So rate each competitive threat statement on a severity scale of one to five, where one means "mildly annoying" and five means "deadly."

Is The Threat Robust?

If a threat can be handled by your routine competitive strategy, it is best to defend against it that way. Reserve strategic defenses for threats that appear to be insufficiently impeded by your routine competitive processes and strategies. If you find yourself with many such threats, then it is time to re-examine your routine competitive processes and strategies to better align them with the realities of the market, not to plan a lot of strategic defenses.

A threat that is essentially unaffected by routine competitive strategy is called robust, and one that is vulnerable to that strategy is called weak. On a scale of one to five, rate the robustness of the threat, where one means "utterly weak" and five means "completely robust."

Is The Threat Credible?

Determining the credibility of a threat is a difficult task. If the competitive threat is a strategic revenue source for the competitor, they are very likely to devote considerable resources to it in the future. This is usually the best yardstick for threat credibility. Credibility is enhanced if the competitor is strong financially and if the offering has or is likely to gain marketplace acceptance.

Credibility may be obvious for existing strategic offerings. Google does not have to wonder about the credibility of the search threats from Yahoo and Microsoft. However, many existing threats evaporate when the competitor loses interest and heads in another direction, goes out of business, or is acquired. If the threat depends on some future action by the competitor, credibility requires careful analysis. Put yourself in the shoes of the competitor's CEO and, considering its profile, ask how likely you would be to take the ongoing action that would produce or sustain the competitive threat.

On the Threat Evaluation Worksheet, rate each competitive threat statement on a scale of one to five, where one means "very unlikely to occur" and five means "certain to occur."

Determine The Cutoff

Now that each competitive threat statement has been rated on severity, robustness, and credibility, it is time to decide on a cutoff point that will determine those you consider strategic, against which you will proceed to craft a strategic defense. It is recommended that you proceed with the threats with a rating of at least four on all three scales. Your judgment may dictate including some others.

Retain the list of items that do not make the strategic cut. It will be used as input into next year's strategic defense planning.

Next, for each surviving strategic threat statement, consider prospective crown jewels to attack.

Step 3:
Select Candidate Crown Jewels To Target

Selecting the crown jewels to target first depends upon whether the threat is an existing offering or a potential one.

- If the threat is an existing offering in its current form, then attack another strategic offering. If the competitor has only one offering and thus nothing else to attack, proceed to step 6-b and select a strategy other than a crown jewels attack.

- If an offering is a threat because of how it might potentially evolve, then attack that offering in its current form or another existing strategic offering.

- If the threat is a potential new offering, then attack an existing strategic offering.

In this framework, an offering is a product or service packaged for a particular market segment. One that is aimed at the general market is an undifferentiated offering; one that is aimed at one or more specific market segments is a differentiated offering. For differentiated offerings, each distinct segment or set of segments presents a separate possible target for you to attack.

For each strategic competitive threat, list the possible crown jewels you could attack on the Candidate Attack Target Worksheet. Ask this question: "If we attacked this offering, would the likely response be for the competitor to divert enough resources away from what we fear that it would remove or significantly reduce the threat to us?" An attack on a strategic revenue source is much more likely to provoke a significant response from the competitor than one on a non-strategic product line.

If you are certain that there are no viable crown jewels to attack, skip to step 6-b.

This step may result in more than one candidate for some threats. At this point, it is fine to have alternatives. Next, develop a prototype for each attack.

Step 4:
Develop Prototype Attacks

In this step, examine each candidate attack target and consider the attack style you would use were you to mount such an attack. The two factors that determine attack style are growth opportunity and desire for control. For each potential attack target on the Candidate Attack Target Worksheet, ask these questions:

- Does this attack present a growth opportunity for us to enhance, develop, or acquire a product line that can make a significant future contribution to our revenue and profit?

- What would be the attack weapon, that is, the product or service offering used to make the attack?

- Do we want to control the attack weapon by owning it?

The answers to these questions determine the attack style, as illustrated in the Attack Style Quadrant, and the attack weapon. Weapon choice and style choice are related. In general, style choice comes first and dictates the constraints on weapon choice. This is a variation of the "find a need and fill it" approach. The need is to divert the competitor's resources away from the strategic threat while meeting your preferences for control and growth opportunity. Weapon choice is then about filling this need with an offering. The form and source of the weapon are otherwise constrained only by other business considerations you may choose to impose. However, while style generally drives weapon choice, an inspired concept for an offering that can be used to attack the competitor's crown jewels may also influence style choice.

	Crown Jewels Attack	
	No Growth	**Growth**
Desire to Control →	Bamboozle Attack	Classic Attack
	Jawbone Attack	Proxy Attack
	Growth Opportunity →	

Own · *Influence*

Attack Style Quadrant
Copyright © 2007 Crown Jewels Group

You can consider a wide range of weapons options. These may range from clone-and-hone to disruptive innovation. In clone-and-hone, you copy the attack target (clone), then modify it by learning from the competitor's mistakes and limitations and, later, your own experience in the market (hone). Microsoft's Zune and Xbox are examples of clone-and-hone offerings. At the other end of the creativity spectrum, a disruptive innovation is an offering that threatens to replace the established competitive offerings in a market. The new offering may lower the price point, simplify the solution or provide other benefit improvements. For example, MP3 players, led by the iPod, have largely replaced a variety of personal music devices, like portable radios and CD players.

You also have the usual build or buy sourcing options and other issues relating to developing a new offering to contemplate. The fine points of an attack weapon are not important at this point. In fact, an attack weapon may evolve as an attack moves towards implementation. So, in this step, flesh out your concept for the attack weapon enough so your team is comfortable with the concept but avoid getting bogged down in details.

Now the task is to develop a prototype attack statement for each attack weapon and style combination. On the following pages, two prototype attack statement formats and examples of each are provided. Use the short attack statement format where brevity is needed and the underlying assumptions are either understood or the level of detail of the long format is not needed. Use the long format when you value more completeness. Which you use on the worksheets is, of course, up to you. In either case, you may want to add a few sentences as needed to clarify or further flesh out the idea for each prototype attack.

The examples of these two attack statement formats refer to the Snick Snack example described earlier in this book. Snick Snack fears that its rival, Mega Cookie, will expand its healthy cookie product line, Mega Bites, marketed to children and their mothers. This would be a strategic threat to Snick Snack's line of healthy treats, Snickys, aimed at the same market. Snick Snack is considering an attack that would target Mega Cookie's other market segment, overweight adults. Note how the market segments of the offerings are carefully described in the examples, since the brand names used by both companies are undifferentiated.

**Attack Statement
Short Format**

We will attack *[attack target]* with *[attack weapon]*. This *[does/does not]* present an opportunity for us to make a significant contribution to our future revenue and profit. We *[do/do not]* want to own and thus control *[attack weapon]*. We will use a *[attack style]*.

**Attack Statement
Long Format**

We will attack *[attack target]* with *[attack weapon]*. The objective is to cause *[competitor's name]* to divert enough resources away from *[strategic threat]* to defend *[attack target]* that the threat of *[strategic threat]* to us will be reduced or eliminated.

This attack *[does/does not]* present an opportunity for us to make a significant contribution to our future revenue and profit. We *[do/do not]* want to own and thus control *[attack weapon]*. We will use a *[attack style]*.

Attack Statement Example
Short Format

We will attack Mega Bites targeted at overweight adults with Snickys targeted at overweight adults. This does present an opportunity for us to make a significant contribution to our future revenue and profit. We do want to own and thus control Snickys targeted at overweight adults. We will use a classic attack.

Snick Snack Attack Statement
Long Format

We will attack Mega Bites targeted at overweight adults with Snickys targeted at overweight adults. The objective is to cause Mega Cookie to divert enough resources away from Mega Bites targeted at children and their mothers to defend Mega Bites targeted at overweight adults that the threat of an expanded line of healthy Mega Cookie treats targeted at children and their mothers will be reduced or eliminated.

This attack does present an opportunity for us to make a significant contribution to our future revenue and profit. We do want to own and thus control Snickys targeted at overweight adults. We will use a classic attack.

At this point, it is possible to have more than one attack weapon and style combination for each crown jewels attack target candidate. Right now, keep them all. For each attack weapon and style combination, write a prototype attack statement on a Strategic Defense Worksheet. Each is evaluated in the next step.

Step 5:
Evaluate Prototype Attacks

At this stage in the strategic competitive defense planning process, you have a list of crown jewel attack targets for each threat. For each attack target, you have one or more prototype attack statements. Now rate each attack statement on strategic fit, net cost, and chance of success.

Strategic Fit

Evaluate how each attack would fit in your company. These considerations include the following:

- Does the attack leverage our strengths?

- Would the attack add strength where we need it?

- Do we have or could we obtain the resources necessary to launch the attack?

- Would the attack be consistent with our branding and image?

- Are there other strategically desirable secondary consequences of the attack?

- Do we have the staying power to continue this attack long enough for it to be successful?

- How does the attack benefit customers, investors, employees, and other stakeholders?

In addition to documenting the answers to these questions, rate each prototype attack for strategic fit on its own Strategic Defense Worksheet using a scale of one to five, where five is a "perfect fit" and one is "no fit at all."

Net Cost

Next, estimate the approximate net cost to the company of each prototype attack. You already know that the threat is severe, robust, and credible, and that there is considerable risk to not mounting an effective defense. Regardless, you must attempt to quantify what it will cost. Experience shows that there are many people who cannot continue with this process or evaluate its results without some financial sizing. A cost and revenue projection for at least three years is useful. The process for estimating net cost is no different for this purpose than for any other endeavor you might evaluate.

Record the result on the Strategic Defense Worksheet and retain the backup documentation of how you arrived at it.

Chance Of Success

The third factor in evaluating each prototype attack is to estimate its chance of succeeding. Success means eliminating the threat or reducing it to the point of being inconsequential. The bottom line question is, do you believe the attack would actually work? Do you believe that the attack would cause the competitor to change its behavior, divert resources away from the strategic threat, and sufficiently reduce the threat or eliminate it entirely? Be sure to carefully consider the competitor's likely response to your attack to be sure the outcome is truly desirable, or that you are at least capable of coping with it.

Rate each prototype attack's chance of success on a scale of one to five, where five is "certain" and one is "not much chance at all." Record the result on the Strategic Defense Worksheet. Also record your assumptions about the likely response of the competitor to the attack.

Select Attacks

For each crown jewels attack target, you now have one or more Strategic Defense Worksheets. Select the best prototype attacks for each target, considering strategic fit, net cost, and chance of success. There may be more than one attack you wish to keep in contention for a particular target. There also may be no viable attack for a target; if that is the case, it will be handled in step 6-b.

Next, consider the other strategic defenses.

Step 6:
Consider Other Defenses

Recall the traditional strategic defenses discussed in part one of this book: Buy Them, Crush Them, Unleash The Lawyers, Erect Barriers To Entry, and Spread FUD. These can be used in two ways. First, except for Buy Them, they can be used to augment a crown jewels attack. Second, they may be substitutes for attacking the crown jewels.

Step 6-a: Consider Augmentation

For each Strategic Defense Worksheet, ask these questions:

- Should we attempt to crush them in addition to attacking them? If so, what vulnerabilities would we attack and how would we attack them? How would this affect strategic fit, net cost, and chance of success?

- Should we unleash the lawyers in addition to attacking them? If so, what legal actions would we pursue? How would this affect strategic fit, net cost, and chance of success?

- Should we erect barriers to entry in addition to attacking them? If so, what specific barriers would we erect? How would this affect strategic fit, net cost, and chance of success?

- Should we spread FUD in addition to attacking them? If so, what would be the themes of our FUD campaign? How would this affect strategic fit, net cost, and chance of success?

Record any of these other defenses that you decide to add to an attack on the Additional Defenses section of the Strategic Defense Worksheet.

Step 6-b: Consider Substitution

For each attack on a Strategic Defense Worksheet, evaluate which, if any, of these other types of defenses should be considered instead of a crown jewels attack. Ask these questions:

- Should we try to buy them instead of attacking them? What would be the strategic fit and approximate net cost?

- Should we attempt to crush them instead of attacking them? If so, what vulnerabilities would we attack and how would we attack them? What would be the strategic fit, net cost, and chance of success?

- Should we unleash the lawyers instead of attacking them? If so, what legal actions would we pursue? What would be the strategic fit, net cost, and chance of success?

- Should we erect barriers to entry instead of attacking them? If so, what specific barriers would we erect? What would be the strategic fit, net cost, and chance of success?

- Should we spread FUD instead of attacking them? If so, what would be the themes of our FUD campaign? What would be the strategic fit, net cost, and chance of success?

If a substitute defensive strategy appears to be a good replacement for a crown jewels attack, document it on a Strategic Defense Worksheet of its own. Then use step 6-a to see if this alternative defense can itself be augmented.

Step 7:
Plan, Decide, Implement

Congratulations! You now have at least one Strategic Defense Worksheet for each strategic threat you intend to act against.

If you still have more than one such worksheet for a particular threat, it is advisable to move each of the alternatives forward so the ultimate decision makers can choose from among them. You may want to use a matrix like the one on the Competitive Defense Alternatives Worksheet to help compare and rank these options as you proceed.

Remember how you got here. Each of these threats is severe, robust, and credible. Combating each now becomes a vital project. Use the same process your company uses for planning and implementing all strategic initiatives for each of these projects. While every organization will have its own way of handling such projects, they all involve fleshing out a plan sufficiently for the necessary decision making to occur, followed by implementation.

The work to defend your strategy against critical threats has just begun. The final chapter of this book presents a set of recommendations regarding how to assure the success of these vital projects. Before that, the next chapter illustrates the process described in this chapter with a case study of a fictional company, Grabonto Corporation.

6

Case Study: Grabonto Corporation

"Tell me and I'll forget. Show me and I may remember.
Involve me and I'll understand." – Chinese proverb

It is Friday morning, and the executive committee of Grabonto Corporation has gathered in the conference room of the resort where they have spent the last week on their annual strategic planning retreat. Grabonto is a three-year old company whose mission is to "make paper documents of all kinds useful in a digital world." They just had their first profitable quarter and forecast $100 million in revenue next year.

Grabonto offers an online service under the brand name ShoeBox. ShoeBox lets you scan documents using a scanner attached to a personal computer, and the documents are stored in your secure, private, online ShoeBox. Your ShoeBox is searchable, but that is just the beginning. ShoeBox automatically extracts data from your document and seamlessly inserts that data into the application of your choice. It uses a vast and growing online database of document types called ShoeBase, along with patented document analysis technology that enables ShoeBox to recognize virtually any document of any size, from a receipt to an insurance document to an invoice, and extract its data.

The other piece of the puzzle is ShoeBox's interoperability technology that it calls ShoeHorn, that works with a vast and growing array of file formats and online and offline computer applications. It seamlessly operates with almost any application, and learns new ones with ease. It inserts data into applications ranging from personal finance software like Quicken and Microsoft Money to big, complex enterprise resource planning systems from companies like Oracle and SAP.

The basic, personal ShoeBox service is free. In exchange for this free service, users must agree to let ShoeBox "learn" when they scan a document it does not recognize. This is how ShoeBox keeps growing its seemingly magical ability to recognize every kind of paper document. There are ShoeBox charges for "extra" services that are aimed at business and government customers who have special storage, security, and backup needs, and per-transaction micro-charges for high volume users, which turns out to be most medium and large sized businesses.

You can also pay a fee and opt-out of the "learn from my documents" program.

C EO Alice Ward takes her seat at the head of the conference table, the signal for everyone else to find a seat and settle in. "I know this has been a tough week," she begins. "I want to thank you all for the hard work you've done and the focus you have brought to our strategic planning. Before we start today's work, I have some great news that may make spending the day at this lovely resort holed up in this room a bit more pleasant."

Grabonto Corporation Executive Committee

Alice Ward, Chief Executive Officer
Brian Chen, Chief Financial Officer
Toni DeMerrit, Chief Technology Officer
Amy Kim, Chief Information Officer
Carl Gomez, Vice President of Marketing
Brent Geller, Vice President of Sales
Diane Nelson, Vice president of Human Resources

"I just got off the phone with our board chairman and we are on course for an IPO in roughly six months." That gets everyone's attention. CFO Brian Chen even closes his laptop, a big smile splitting his usually serious face. "I know this raises lots of question, and we will have a full briefing on the IPO plan a week from Monday, so clear your calendars for that day. I'll have the location of that meeting tonight. Now I need you to focus on today's tasks."

"Yesterday, we started our work on competitive threats. Up to now, we have been sailing on the proverbial blue ocean, with no real competition. That can't last forever, and I'd rather be proactive than reactive. So this is very important to me." Alice makes eye-contact with each person around the table in turn. "OK, we gave Carl the honor of being our record keeper, so I'd like him to summarize what we've accomplished so far. Its all yours, Carl."

Carl Gomez, vice president of marketing, moves to the easel at the front of the room and flips to a page labeled "threat evaluation worksheet." "The first thing we did yesterday was agree that our routine strategy should handle all of the scanner manufacturers, at least for the next three years. We have good partnership agreements with most of them and support all of them. We rated the threat as pretty severe but not very robust or credible."

"Next, we considered the document management companies as a group. We have partnership agreements with all the major ones and many of the smaller ones. We feed their systems our data, exchange technical information with them, and are neutral among them. Again, our routine strategy seems to be working. So we also rated this threat as moderately severe but not robust or credible."

"We also agreed that Toni and I need to constantly review the threats posed by the scanner and document management folks, as if we didn't already know that! Our intellectual property protection, partnership contracts, and R&D plans will protect us from both of these threats, right Toni?" Everyone laughs, including chief technology officer Toni DeMerrit, who gets up and takes a little bow.

"Now we come to the company we are really worried about, UnBabel." Carl scowls as he continues. "These guys are a real threat."

Threat Evaluation Worksheet Steps 1 and 2			
Threat Statement	**Severe (1–5)**	**Robust (1–5)**	**Credible (1–5)**
The other scanning companies are a potential threats if they decide to develop ShoeBox clones.	4	2	2
The document management companies are a potential threat if they decide to develop ShoeBox clones.	4	2	2
UnBabel's interoperation tools are a threat if they add document recognition technology and build a service that competes with ShoeBox.	5	3	4

"UnBabel is in the business of providing middleware between disparate business systems, like Oracle, SAP, and Microsoft business applications. They've been at this a lot longer than we have and are much bigger, and they have an extensive capability to insert data into applications.

What we fear is that UnBabel could add document recognition technology and build a very competitive offering. Their size would give them instant credibility in a very profitable high-end segment of our market, though they'd likely stay away from the home and small and medium-sized business markets."

Carl tapes a worksheet to the wall. "Here is the strategic profile of UnBabel. We rated this threat as severe, somewhat credible, and pretty darn robust. We decided to treat this threat as a strategic one even though we rated the credibility as a three, just below the cutoff we'd usually use. The reasoning behind the credibility rating was that we have no good reading on their new CEO. There is a lot of talk that he was brought in to get the company acquired. Still, these guys make us all nervous." Nods and a few wan smiles materialize around the table.

"UnBabel has two revenue streams, both of which are strategic. They make 60% of their revenue, about $360 million this year, from UnKit. This is a set of web services linked to what UnBabel calls their interoperability knowledgebase. Customers license UnKit and use it to connect their applications. The second product line is UnEasy, which is a product built over UnKit that customers license to migrate data when they change applications. They also wrap service around this for turnkey migrations. The revenue from this was about $240 million this year. So we have two crown jewels to consider attacking."

Carl takes his seat and Alice says, "OK, this is a good time for a break. We'll look at prototype attacks after the break. Everyone back in 20 minutes."

**Strategic Competitor Profile Worksheet
Step 2**

Competitor: UnBabel Technology Corporation

Mission Statement: "We make a customer's business applications work together. We do this by seamlessly exchanging data among applications behind the scenes."

Key Strengths:
1. excellent direct sales force
2. strong patent portfolio
3. large interoperability database
4. large number of partnerships
5. solid R&D
6. large customer base

Key Weaknesses:
1. poor after-sale customer support
2. overly aggressive sales force
3. recent key executive turnover

Revenue Sources:
UnKit: $360 million
UnEasy: $240 million

After the break, Alice says, "We broke up into two teams yesterday afternoon. Toni, Brent, and Diane were assigned to plan the attack on UnKit. Amy, Brian, and Carl worked on UnEasy." Alice smiles broadly. "Now I can admit that while you were all working on that, I got to sneak off and work on the IPO plan. OK, Amy, how about your team going first?"

Chief information officer Amy Kim gets up and moves to the easel. Turning the flip chart to the next sheet, she says, "We got stuck right away on the question of which style to use. It was Brian's fault. Being chief financial officer, he wanted lots of revenue but no cost." Brian joins in the good-natured laughter."

Candidate Attack Target Worksheet Step 3	
Threat Statement	**Crown Jewels Target**
UnBabel's interoperation tools are a threat to ShoeBox if they add document recognition technology and build a service that competes with ShoeBox.	UnKit, their web services and knowledgebase suite for interoperation
UnBabel's interoperation tools are a threat to ShoeBox if they add document recognition technology and build a service that competes with ShoeBox.	UnEasy, their product to move data from one or more applications to others

"Seriously," Amy continues, "the first thing we did was dismiss the services side of the UnEasy business. They already have plenty of competition from IBM and Accenture and others who even use the UnEasy product to deliver migration services. We hear that both IBM and Accenture make several times as much from this as UnBabel does.

We're pretty sure UnBabel is not too concerned strategically about the services revenue, and even if they were, anything we did would not add enough to the competition to matter."

Crown Jewels Attack

	No Growth	Growth	
Desire to Control →	Bamboozle Attack	Classic Attack	**Own**
	Jawbone Attack	Proxy Attack	**Influence**

Growth Opportunity →

Attack Style Quadrant
Copyright © 2007 Crown Jewels Group

Amy tapes up a sheet with the Attack Style Quadrant on it and says, "But we do think an attack on the UnEasy product could work. To figure out the attack style, we first asked if we wanted growth from this. Brian was adamant that we should try for that. Then Carl convinced us that that this sort of data migration product was far afield from our mission and we should not try to control it through ownership because that could get us off course. So we wanted growth without control and started looking for a proxy attack."

Amy sips some water, then says, "Our idea is to leverage our database of information about applications and file formats, ShoeBase, and the software we have to insert data into all the various applications, ShoeHorn. We'd create a kit of web services tools that third parties can use to access this stuff and build applications. For now, we've called this ShoeFit." Some good natured moans come from around the table. "Then we find a proxy to build the attack weapon, an UnEasy clone, using ShoeFit. Carl figures there are a number of ways we can monetize ShoeFit, and there is already something like it on our product roadmap, but a few years out. We'd just accelerate it."

Amy pauses for another sip of water. "Now," she says, "for the fun part. We make money from ShoeFit but we are not in direct competition with UnBabel. Our proxy who builds the UnEasy clone is their threat! We need a proxy to build the weapon and go after that market. Want to speak to that, Carl?"

"Sure," Carl says, "it just so happens that I've been approached by two companies who want access to ShoeBase and ShoeHorn for interoperability products. I'm pretty sure that both are serious. Since no one has anything like ShoeBase and ShoeHorn, I think they or someone else will be a decent proxy."

"We can use a variety of inducements to influence a proxy, especially if our IPO is successful. And I believe that a decent attack on UnEasy will get UnBabel's attention and pin down their resources defending it, just like we want, especially if they are trying to pretty-up the picture for an acquisition."

Strategic Defense Worksheet Steps 4, 5 and 6	
Threat Statement: UnBabel's interoperation tools are a threat to ShoeBox if they add document recognition technology and build a service that competes with ShoeBox.	
Attack Statement: We will attack UnEasy with a clone built around Shoe-Fit, a new web service for accessing ShoeBase and ShoeHorn. ShoeFit presents an opportunity for us to make a significant contribution to our future revenue and profit. We do not want to own and thus control the UnEasy clone, but we will own ShoeFit. We will use a proxy attack.	
Strategic Fit (1-5): 5	**Chance Of Success: (1-5):** 4
Net Cost:	
Additional Defenses:	
Likely Response:	

Amy turns to the flipchart to the next sheet and says, "Thanks, Carl. So here is how we see the attack. We've rated the fit a five and the chance of success a four, mainly because five seemed a bit overconfident." Amy sits down.

"Great job," says Alice. "Questions? Discussion?"

"What about the cost?" asks Diane Nelson, vice president of human resources. "How'd you leave that out with Brian on your team?"

"Well," Brian says, "we wanted Toni's input on the development cost. What would it take, Toni?"

"Assuming we don't want to disrupt our current development activity, figure $250,000 with a nine-month lead time for a first release," Toni says. "And plan on the same amount annually for ongoing maintenance and so forth."

"Add $150,000 annually for marketing," says Carl. "I did some back-of-the-envelope estimates on the revenue side and, being conservative, I'd plan on no revenue for year one, with a linear ramp up to $25 million in three years. Most of that would come from transaction fees for ShoeBase access, just like we get from other volume users."

"Anything else on cost?" asks Alice. "No? Brian, would you please pull together the numbers from Toni and Carl and do your messaging of them for this fiscal year and the following two years? Then send us all a spreadsheet by Monday?" Brian nods. "Thanks," says Alice, "any more discussion?"

For the next 45 minutes, the group talks over the proposed attack on UnEasy. As the conversation winds down, Alice announces that lunch time has arrived, adding, "we'll hear from the other team after lunch."

When everyone has returned from the lunch break, Brent Geller, vice president of sales, moves to the front of the room. "Oddly," he says, with a mock look of puzzlement on his face, "our team chose the sales guy as spokesman. Go figure!"

"We looked at how to attack UnBabel's UnKit product," Brent continues. "UnKit has a lot of similarity to the combination of ShoeBase and ShoeHorn. We use them to insert data from documents into applications. You use UnKit to move data between applications. Seems pretty similar to me, which I guess is why we fear them moving onto our turf. As most of you probably know, I've brought in deals where commercial customers want to use Shoe-Base and ShoeHorn just like UnKit. They'd rather deal with one vendor than two. The answer from Alice has always been a 'no' because we've wanted to stay focused on our document processing mission."

"Well, Diane and I asked Toni why we shouldn't consider expanding our mission. I know we spent a lot of time at the beginning of the week focused on our strategic plans for paper document handling, and we have a great and innovative roadmap. But here we have this great technology and we are missing a great market for it. We may have gotten started with documents where we had pretty much an uncontested blue ocean, but now that we are well established, let's take the gloves off and really attack UnBabel!" Brent pumps his fist in the air, then says, "So tell them your thoughts, Toni."

"After you guys stroked my ego about our great technology, I realized that I have been so focused on document processing since we started the company that I may have become myopic," says Toni. "Alice and I had this vision of making life easy for people who would normally throw their receipts and so forth in a shoe box. That led to the technology ideas. Then we expanded the vision to businesses so we could make some real money. We actually have a very short road to travel technically to move right into UnBabel's market. We never planned for that, but the very technology we needed got us here. I for one am open to the idea."

Brent flips the chart on the easel and says, "So, we figure we should try a classic attack. You know, growth and control. Here is what we came up with. It sure looks a lot like the other team's idea. That's why I like to go first to pitch a deal, then you get to shape the discussion and take credit for all the ideas you present."

Toni says, "Now you see why I had the $250,000 development cost on the tip of my tongue earlier. We stopped there, figuring Carl should work on the rest of the cost and revenue. If we go after the UnBabel market full tilt, the ongoing costs for R&D will surely be higher."

Diane chimes in, "We were neutral about strategic fit. You could say it's a bad fit to our current strategy or a great fit if we revise our strategy as Brent and Toni were saying. Oh, and we didn't give the attack weapon a code name or anything. We know how much fun Carl has with that sort of thing and didn't want to step on his toes. It is a sort of ShoeFit idea, just more specific to the UnKit market."

Alice stands up and says, "I think this calls for another 20 minute break. It seems we have a lot to think about and talk over. This is all most interesting."

Strategic Defense Worksheet Steps 4, 5 and 6	
Threat Statement: UnBabel's interoperation tools are a threat to ShoeBox if they add document recognition technology and build a service that competes with ShoeBox.	
Attack Statement: We will attack UnKit head-on by building a web service for exchanging data between applications. This new product will use ShoeBase and ShoeHorn. This presents an opportunity for us to make a significant contribution to our future revenue and profit. We want to own and thus control the attack weapon. We will use a classic attack.	
Strategic Fit (1-5): 3	**Chance Of Success: (1-5):** 4
Net Cost: $250k for R&D first year	
Additional Defenses:	
Likely Response:	

After the break, Alice says, "I know some of you are nervous about how I might react to the idea of enlarging our overall strategy to encompass application integration. I have been pretty rigid about staying focused on our original mission. I still think that focus is what got us here, but I don't want to inhibit this discussion. So let's forge on. The decision making comes later."

Brian Chen says, "I assume you want me to work up the numbers for this plan as well as the other one." Alice nods agreement. "No problem," says Brian.

For the next hour, the group discusses the idea Brent presented. During that discussion, Diane wonders out loud about possibly using a bamboozle attack on UnKit as a way to get started, with the option of moving to a classic style attack later. She thinks Grabonto could use its friends in the analyst community to hype the threat to UnBabel and do just enough R&D work to make the threat seem plausible to UnBabel. Brian says he thinks that would be too tentative a move, while Carl says that it could be used as a sort of exploratory attack while the direct attack was being planned in detail.

Then Alice says, "I think it's time to move on. I'd like to summarize. We have two strategic defenses proposed, one that targets each of UnBabel's two crown jewels. In both cases, we agree that the attack should be augmented by more focused and targeted work on our patent portfolio and any other intellectual property barriers we can erect."

"Brent is going to run the numbers for both of these so we have them Monday. Toni and Carl, I'd like you to work together and flesh out both of the Strategic Defense Worksheets with some supporting detail. Look ahead three years. I know it's a stretch, but can you get that done for Monday as well?" Both nod.

Competitive Defense Alternatives Worksheet Step 7			
Threat Statement: UnBabel's interoperation tools are a threat to ShoeBox if they add document recognition technology and build a service that competes with ShoeBox.			
	Strategic Fit ---------- **Chance Of Success**	**Net Cost**	**Rank**
Classic attack on UnKit	3		
Likely Response:	4		
Bamboozle attack on UnKit	3		
Likely Response:	2		
Classic attack on UnEasy	5		
Likely Response:	4		

"I also want to look at Diane's suggestion of a bamboozle attack on UnKit. Even though my hunch is that the chance of success for that is at best a two, I want to explore it a bit further. So I'm asking Toni, Carl, and Brian to work up this third plan as well."

Alice goes to the flipchart and fills in the Competitive Defense Alternatives Worksheet. "Here are the alternatives you'll be working on. Be sure to include the likely responses that were mentioned during our discussions today."

"It seems to me that we will come out of this with a solid defense against the threat from UnBabel. I want to use our regular Tuesday morning staff meeting to review and rank these alternatives and make a decision about what we recommend to the board of directors."

Alice smiles broadly as she makes eye contact with each person in the room. "This has been a great meeting, and I appreciate the level of the discussion. We've accomplished what I hoped for and then some. So unless there are any objections, I move we adjourn to the bar. After that, you're on your own. I know some of you are staying until tomorrow to take advantage of the golf course. I know I am!"

This fictional account of Grabonto Corporation's executive committee meeting illustrates how to use the strategic competitive defense planning process. You may want to think about the following questions:

- How well did the strategic competitive defense planning process work for Grabonto?

- What would you have done differently in this meeting?

- What do you imagine UnBabel's response would be to each of these crown jewel attacks?

- What do you think about the discussion regarding possibly enlarging Grabonto's overall strategy to encompass application integration?

- What do you think Grabonto will decide to do? Why?

It is often hard to strike the right balance between being a meeting facilitator and being a participant. CEO Alice Ward did a good job of this. She kept the group focused, moved the discussion along and kept herself in the background. In doing so, she may have sacrificed her ability to be a full participant. Perhaps Alice did this as a matter of personal style, preferring to lead by listening more than by talking. She and her team also seemed very comfortable with the strategic competitive defense planning process, which made her facilitating role straightforward. However, it is often more effective to have this kind of meeting run by a facilitator who is experienced in the specific process, rather than in the organization's specific business. This person can be a neutral force, keeping the meeting moving along and on-track, clarifying process issues that emerge and allowing everyone to participate fully, including the CEO.

As you read the next chapter on assuring attack success, you may want to imagine that you are Grabonto's CEO and envision how you would proceed to assure that the UnBabel threat is successfully attacked and constrained.

7

Assuring Attack Success

"Vision without execution is delusion."
– Peter Drucker

You and your team have completed your annual strategic competitive defense planning process. You have identified a strategic competitive threat and developed a rough plan to defend against it. Now comes the hard work of fleshing out the details of that plan and then turning it into action. This is a critical transition during which much can go wrong and the good intentions of those involved in the initial planning activity can easily be thwarted.

This seems like the usual progression from high-level plan to implementation project. But this is no ordinary project. Because this new endeavor has at its core the objective of defending your business strategy, it is itself a strategic initiative, one that is essential to the future of the business. This project needs to be effective for a long period of time. It must stay focused on the objective of diverting your competitor's resources to avert the strategic threat. This is no easy matter as such a major initiative evolves over time, many people become involved, and meeting other business needs expands its objectives.

CEOs recognize that attention to strategy is vital to an organization's long term success. That's all well and good, but the compelling, relentless immediacy of operational problems and the need to produce quarterly results makes routine attention to strategic initiatives difficult. This is the main reason why these projects often fail. Suddenly, it seems, a year has gone by and not much progress has been made defending against a threat that was and still is severe, robust, and credible.

This chapter recommends a checklist of specific actions a CEO can take to assure that a crown jewels attack and other strategic defenses succeed, regardless of these pressures. Not surprisingly, most of these measures are essential to the successful outcome of strategic initiatives in general as well as strategic defenses specifically.

This final chapter concludes with some closing words about instilling the crown jewels philosophy into an organization's culture.

CEOs Checklist

The checklist of recommended action items that a CEO can use to guide a strategic defensive initiative to success are listed in the following chart. They are then individually described in more detail.

**Assuring Attack Success
Checklist**

✓ Sanity Check
✓ Align The Message With An Inspirational Vision
✓ Create A Sense Of Urgency
✓ Assign Project Leader Responsibility And Authority
✓ Schedule Periodic CEO Reviews
✓ Schedule Board Reviews
✓ Schedule The Annual Planning Process
✓ Budget Realistically
✓ Establish Metrics
✓ Staff Properly
✓ Align Compensation

Sanity Check

Begin with a sanity check. Any organization can only handle a limited number of strategic initiatives at any one time. How many depends on organization size and the strength of senior management. There is no right number. If, however, you find that the number of strategic initiatives facing your organization seems excessive, review and prune the list to a manageable size. Nothing can crush an organization's morale and trust in management quite as much as lofty strategic visions, announced with great fanfare, that vaporize.

With any new major initiative, the organization takes its cues from the CEO with regard to the seriousness of the organization's commitment. Everyone needs to believe that this is not just another flavor-of-the-month bright idea. In a manner consistent with the CEO's personal style, the CEO ideally serves as the cheerleader-in-chief for the initiative on an ongoing basis. As part of the sanity check, then, be certain the CEO is fully committed and willing to display that commitment to the organization on a sustained basis.

The nature of the specific initiative may require some secrecy until it is ready for a full rollout. You may not want to tip your hand until the project is at a certain point. Regardless, as more and more people are brought into the picture, they must know that the CEO is absolutely serious about this. This message is best heard when it is delivered directly, personally, and repeatedly by the CEO.

Align The Message With An Inspirational Vision

Every strategic initiative can and should be expressed with a vision statement that sets a clear, bold, compelling, even audacious reason for its very existence. For example, when Microsoft launched Xbox, Bill Gates said, "building on our strengths as a software company, Xbox will offer game developers a powerful platform and game enthusiasts an incredible experience. We want Xbox to be the platform of choice for the best and most creative game developers in the world."

The vision statement does not describe the complex process by which the company came to the decision to commit to the initiative. That reasoning may have been driven by a number of converging factors, such as the needs to defend against a competitive threat, increase revenue with a new venture in a growth market, and assert leadership in an emerging category. Regardless of the motivation, the outcome of those needs is an offering that has significant benefits to customers. This is the fore-ground message. This is the vision that can excite and motivate people. This is the message to use internally and externally.

By meeting customer needs with those benefits, the company expects to meet other goals, like growing finan-cially and warding off a serious competitive threat. These, however, are background messages. They may be impor-tant to selective audiences, like the board of directors and investors. They are not what energizes the organization or the public. Thus, Microsoft's Xbox announcement con-tained not a word about keeping Sony PlayStation in check.

If you use a formal strategic competitive defense plan-ning process like the one in this book, an essential step is the strategic fit analysis. Recall the following questions that were suggested for this in chapter five:

- Does the attack leverage our strengths?

- Would the attack add strength where we need it?

- Do we have or could we obtain the resources necessary to launch the attack?

- Would the attack be consistent with our branding and image?

- Are there other strategically desirable secondary consequences of the attack?

- Do we have the staying power to continue this attack long enough for it to be successful?

- How does the attack benefit customers, investors, employees, and other stakeholders?

For attacks that go forward, the answers to these questions is where the formulation of the ultimate rationale begins. It will almost never simply be, "we are doing thus-and-so to defend our widgets against those so-and-sos." The sooner this message starts to take form and becomes part of what everyone hears about the idea, the better. In particular, if the CEO is to stay on message, that message needs to exist explicitly and have stability. Though it can be refined, do not fundamentally change it or it will lose credibility.

One problem a well crafted, motivating, visionary message poses is that sometimes the company forgets why it really did something in the first place, the so-called underlying or "real" reasons. While this kind of organizational memory loss is not confined to strategic initiatives, it can be deadly when it causes one to go off track or be terminated without accomplishing the original core mission. Use the annual strategic competitive defense planning process and board oversight to prevent this, and CEO continuity certainly helps as well.

Create A Sense Of Urgency

A new strategic initiative is constantly in conflict with the inertia of business-as-usual. To combat this, create and reinforce an ongoing sense of urgency. This means that deadlines large and small need to be set, monitored, and held sacred.

The vision message is often the place to set one or more major deadlines. Consider this passage from President John F. Kennedy's speech entitled "Special Message To Congress On Urgent National Needs" delivered in 1961:

"I believe that this nation should commit itself to achieving the goal, before this decade is out, of landing a man on the moon and returning him safely to the earth. No single space project in this period will be more impressive to mankind, or more important for the long-range exploration of space; and none will be so difficult or expensive to accomplish. We propose to accelerate the development of the appropriate lunar space craft. We propose to develop alternate liquid and solid fuel boosters, much larger than any now being developed, until certain which is superior. We propose additional funds for other engine development and for unmanned explorations—explorations which are par-

ticularly important for one purpose which this nation will never overlook: the survival of the man
who first makes this daring flight. But in a very real
sense, it will not be one man going to the moon—if
we make this judgment affirmatively, it will be an
entire nation. For all of us must work to put him
there."

The very title of the speech explicitly establishes the
urgency. The first sentence sets the bold vision and overarching deadline. The challenge is then laid out with a
series of milestone events. This stirring message launched
the American nation on the path to a remarkable achievement, the 1969 Apollo 11 mission that saw Neil Armstrong
and Edwin 'Buzz' Aldrin walk on the moon and return
safely to earth.

Deadlines are discussed further below, in the context of
project metrics.

Assign Project Leader Responsibility And Authority

As early as possible, assign one senior executive overall
project responsibility and authority. This is the person with
bottom-line accountability. Who that should be varies
depending upon the nature of the project and the available
talent pool. Avoid the temptation to push this assignment
too far down the executive ranks. Sure, everyone's plate is
already full, but this is not about balancing workload, it is
about who is the best person to get the job done. For a
strategic initiative, that best person is a high-level, highly
respected executive in their prime. This is not an assign-

ment for a rising star unless you are certain they are ready for it and that the organization is ready to follow them. It is also not a place to park an executive who is coasting toward impending retirement.

One sure sign that you have selected the wrong person is if they ask, "What is the priority of this project?" This is said by someone who has not realized that the job of an executive is to deliver on a number of major objectives, all of which are top priority. This is someone who does not appreciate the meaning of the word strategic in strategic initiative.

It is not enough to hold this person accountable for the progress and success of the initiative. They must also have the authority to get the job done. Assigning responsibility without commensurate authority simply creates a victim. This means personally assuring that all key staff are clear about the project leader's authority. It goes beyond briefing your executive team on the project and announcing who you have put in charge.

In every organization, there are key executives and others who can make or break an initiative. They control vital resources and processes that must accommodate the initiative, or influence those who do. They have their own pressures, priorities, and ambitions. They need to hear directly from the CEO that the CEO wants and needs their full support of the project and its leader. They need to hear from the CEO that the success of this initiative is now one of their explicit objectives. They need to hear from the CEO that this is a number one priority for each of them. This goes beyond getting buy-in, it is about getting clarity of command commitment.

Schedule Periodic CEO Reviews

Nothing says the company is serious about something quite so much as when meetings about it with the CEO get on people's calendars and the CEO makes sure the meetings actually happen. As soon as project leadership is assigned, schedule monthly progress review meetings with the CEO for the next year. Written reports are fine, but they are not substitutes for face-to-face discussions. Then stick to your schedule.

Schedule Board Reviews

Tracking the status of strategic initiatives is a core board of director's responsibility. Make a progress report on all strategic initiatives a standing item on the board's agenda. Ideally, the project leader prepares the summary report for the board and briefs it.

Schedule The Annual Planning Process

Unlike the other items on the CEO checklist that apply to the success of strategic initiatives in general, this one is specific to strategic defense projects. It is to make the strategic competitive defense planning process an annual event. Schedule this before or as a part of the annual budget process. If you do a full strategic planning review, make this a part of it. Throw all prior strategic defense initiatives back into the hopper to assure that the threat continues to merit the initiative continuing and that the initiative remains on track towards its initial objective. Of course, classic and proxy attacks that create offerings that become growth engines for the business are likely to continue long after the threat that instigated them is no longer an issue.

Budget Realistically

Throughout the project's duration, the CEO must assure that that the project has sufficient budget. There is no surer signal that the company is not serious than an inadequate budget. This CEO attention is particularly important in the first year of the project, to give it momentum and get it off to a great start. Insist on reviewing the start-up budget jointly with the project leader and the CFO.

Establish Metrics

Another item on the agenda of the CEO's project kickoff meeting with the project leader and the CFO is the need to establish measurements that allow management to accurately gauge the progress of the initiative on an ongoing basis. Create a project "dashboard" that puts key metrics at the fingertips of all those who need them, with the level of detail appropriate to each job function. This is a classic case of "what gets measured gets done."

An essential part of measuring progress is the achievement of deadlines, major and minor, as discussed above from the perspective of creating a sense of urgency. The CEO sets the mega-milestones and the project leader drives those down into the organization with sufficient detail to keep everyone focused. Make progress against these deadlines part of the project metrics.

Staff Properly

The CEO must assure that the project leader can recruit key members of the project team from various parts of the company. Avoid the common pitfall of staffing the project with castoffs. The right people will be top performers who will be sorely missed by their managers and there will be pushback and resentment in many quarters if this is not dealt with properly. Meet with the project leader and the head of human resources together to discuss how this will be handled.

Align Compensation

Few thing focus the mind better than compensation. It is for many the ultimate motivating measurement system. As the project roles out, be sure that the compensation of those involved delivers the right message.

- For executives whose support is vital, add objectives related to their specific contribution to the project's success to the formula for their bonuses.

- For key project staff, be sure that their base and variable compensation are aligned with their level of responsibility and the project's success.

- For anyone who is commissioned and whose behavior influences the projects success, assure that their commission structure motivates the desired behavior. It is remarkable how often a new initiative flounders because sales staff can make more money if they spend their time selling the old offerings instead of the new one.

Cover these compensation issues as part of the agenda of the CEO's project kickoff meeting with the project leader and the head of human resources.

The Crown Jewels Culture

The foundation of the crown jewels attack strategy is a powerful set of guiding principals for dealing with competitive strategic threats. These principals can be used to build a *crown jewels culture* that effectively deals with such threats routinely and in a timely manner, and often grows the business while doing so.

In a crown jewels culture, strategic competitive threats are identified early by processes embedded in routine management activity. Comprehensive plans are developed to combat these threats. Those plans are implemented with enduring, visible commitment, excitement and an ongoing sense of urgency emanating from the top of the organization. They are managed, monitored, and resourced in a manner that maximizes their chances to succeed.

A crown jewels culture promotes the shared notion that threats should always be viewed as growth opportunities. Soberly facing the reality of competitive threats, the organization embraces the philosophy: "When life gives you lemons, make lemonade. And make money doing it!" It seizes these opportunities, embraces their challenges and thrives on the excitement of conquering new frontiers. With each success doing this, the organization increases its confidence and competence in handling strategic competitive threats. Thus, success breeds success.

One trait shared by enduringly successful companies is that they proactively defend their strategic plans from forces that could derail them. They do not rely on hope. They do not seek the comfort of denial. Year-in and year-out, they aggressively combat strategic competitive threats. They embody a crown jewels culture. You are cordially invited to join their ranks.

Protect your crown jewels—attack theirs!

Acknowledgements

The seeds for this book were planted well over a decade ago by four visionary thinkers, Michael Porter, Michel Robert, Geoffrey Moore, and Ichak Adizes. Their writings and presentations stimulated me to think strategically about business and to look for patterns and models that explained both successful and unsuccessful behavior by companies. I am thankful to them for opening my eyes and my mind.

My deepest gratitude goes to Lois Bookman and Lenny Greenberg, who were with me every step of the way as this book evolved. They suffered through multiple drafts with thoughtful patience and timely responsiveness, and helped me to get details right, elaborate where I was cryptic, cut where I was pointlessly verbose, tighten up my use of language and put my thoughts in a coherent order. Lenny's point of view as a technology strategist was especially useful in fine-tuning the models.

I want to thank a number of people who helped me round out my presentation by offering their professional perspectives. Marketing maven Wayne Caccamo contributed valuable insights on messaging, which included the title of this book. He also helped me sharpen the examples and use consistent, clear terminology. Vikas Joshi generously shared his strategic viewpoint and challenged me to address a number of important business issues. Rick Koski gave me the reality check of a seasoned operations executive and process expert. Noah Bookman prodded me to be more rigorous in the models and process details.

Some of the ideas presented in this book were first formulated in posts on my blog. I greatly appreciate all the blog readers who have provided feedback. It has sharpened and expanded my thinking. I am especially grateful to my sons: Matthew, who implored me to "start writing now," and Bruce, whose thoughts on my blog posts keep me on my toes. You both inspire me every day.

Index

About The Author

Phil Bookman is CEO of the Crown Jewels Group, his business strategy consulting company. A Silicon Valley veteran with a long record of starting, growing, and managing profitable software companies, he developed a unique style of dealing with competition and strategy that is direct, clear, and practical. The attacking the crown jewels model and the Strategic Competitive Defense Planning[SM] process grew out of this, blended with insights gained from observing, analyzing, and participating in the high-tech industry for three decades.

Phil is a member of the Association for Strategic Planning, the Society of Competitive Intelligence Professionals, the American Management Association, and the Chief Operating Officer Business Forum. A graduate of Rensselaer Polytechnic Institute, Adelphi University, and Santa Clara University, he lives with his wife, Lois, in Los Gatos, California.

For More Information About
Attacking The Crown Jewels

Visit the web site below to order copies of *Attacking The Crown Jewels,* to find out more about how you can use the Strategic Competitive Defense Planning[SM] process in your organization, or to give us feedback, which is welcomed. You can also download copies of the worksheets and other reference material from this site.

www.AttackingTheCrownJewels.com